AWARDS FOR GOOD BOYS

Shelby Lorman is a writer, illustrator and comedian from Los Angeles. She thinks and writes about modern dating, technological mishaps and our dystopian present, and created the Instagram account @awardsforgoodboys. She lives in New York with her dog Clem.

AWARDS FOR GOOD BOYS

TALES OF DATING, DOUBLE STANDARDS AND DOOM

SHELBY LORMAN

HUTCHINSON
LONDON

1 3 5 7 9 10 8 6 4 2

Hutchinson
20 Vauxhall Bridge Road
London SW1V 2SA

Hutchinson is part of the Penguin Random House group of companies whose addresses can be
found at global.penguinrandomhouse.com

Copyright © Shelby D. Lorman 2019

Shelby Lorman has asserted her right under the
Copyright, Designs and Patents Act, 1988,
to be identified as the author of this work.

First published in the United States by Penguin Books in 2019
First published in the United Kingdom by Hutchinson in 2019

Some of the selections in this book first appeared in different form on Instagram.

www.penguin.co.uk

A CIP catalogue record for this book is available from the British Library.

ISBN 9781786332264

Text design by Sabrina Bowers

Printed and bound by LEGO

Penguin Random House is committed to a sustainable future for our business, our readers and
our planet. This book is made from Forest Stewardship Council® certified paper.

To Shirley and Clementine

CONTENTS

WTF IS THIS BOOK?

I took a Tinder date back to my apartment while writing this book. This was a bad idea.

For a moment he was flying, held aloft by the authority afforded to a boy like him—straight, white, cis. But my room was the sun. Rest in peace, sweet Icarus.

The walls of my room were plastered with drawings of awards—medals, laurel leaves, trophies—commending men for just barely eking above our collectively low standards for them. In one corner, my detective-trope dreams are fulfilled, with actual pieces of red string connecting suspects like "sonic manspreading" and "things men have said to me after I've set boundaries." And my pièce de résistance: a mountain of printed-out and annotated Tinder conversations. Right there on my desk. *Annotated. Tinder. Conversations.* Nice to meet you, too, Tinder Stranger, oh-did-I-mention-I'm-writing-a-book-about-good-boys-of-which-you-are-one-have-a-great-night!

His face was like: what the fuck?

Which is a really good question. What the fuck?

So . . . I give awards to good boys. It's that literal. I co-opted language from the Dog World to describe the praise we heap on men for meeting the barest of minimums, for avoiding being the Outright Worst.

good·boy /good boi /
noun

A MAN WHO WOULD NEVER DO ANYTHING EXPLICITLY "BAD" (BY HIS OWN MEASURE) BUT, CONSCIOUSLY OR NOT, USES HIS "GOODNESS" AS A SHIELD BEHIND WHICH HE CAN GET AWAY WITH STILL-PRETTY-BAD BEHAVIOR ON THE GROUNDS THAT IT'S NOT OUTWARDLY HORRIFIC

I look at how men are put on literal and figurative pedestals in public spheres and—crucially—in our private lives for, again, achieving what should be THE BASELINE FOR HUMAN DECENCY. I use humor to do so because (1) I'm hilarious and (2) HOLY SHIT WE DESERVE TO LAUGH RIGHT NOW.

Some of you reading, hopefully, will be able to use what I make as a way to offload some of the emotional labor involved in walking people, especially men, through why their self-proclaimed goodness isn't actually so great. To validate your perhaps still unspoken suspicions, to reiterate that, though our experiences are unique, you're not alone.

Some of you might feel more like my Tinder date did when he looked at my walls: a mixture of panic and fear and WTF IS HAPPENING? THIS ISN'T AS SEXY AS I THOUGHT IT WOULD BE!

But look: in order to grow, we must first all become that Tinder date, wandering unsuspecting into the den of my bedroom. We must confront this messiness, the raw material, the strings on the walls, and piece together how these dynamics manifest in our own lives. It's complicated. But that's where I'll be spelunking: into the murky depths of attempting to name the not outwardly bad but not quite good we might not have the words for yet. I'm exploring the fathoms of the hell that is living in the world while being treated as "woman"—a journey, in our case, that will take us down a road paved with good intentions and some very, very good boys.

THE
INSTANT - NEXT

MTV used to have a brutal dating show called *NEXT*. The show (compared to, say, *The Bachelor*) didn't even gesture at future romance between the contestants, as was evident in the very premise. It was speed dating of a grim variety: eligible dates waited in *a tour bus* that trailed behind the "NEXTER" who could, at any minute, say-slash-scream the titular phrase to someone they were, at that moment, on a date with, sending the reject back to the tour bus as another person seamlessly emerged for their own hellish debutante date entrance, complete with freeze-frame "fun facts" that seemed to be written by a bot.

CANDACE, 22

- CAN FART
- ONCE SET HER PET HAMSTER LOOSE IN PETCO AND TOLD MANAGEMENT THERE WAS A ROAMING HAMSTER LOOSE
- LOVES THE SUN

If the tour bus date wasn't Nexted, they were offered a second date or the option to take the money—oh yeah, they've been counting this whole time, you get a dollar per minute spent on the date, everyone really wants to be here—and run.

There was no great way to say "NEXT" to the person you were, at that moment, on a date with.

But there was a particularly bad way: the instant-Next. In these tragic instances, the date would barely make it down the steps before a bellowed "NEXT" forced them back inside. It was the public version of swiping left on someone via Tinder. The performance of (likely arbitrary) judgment—and rejection—that we are usually, blessedly, spared from.

• • •

I was instant-Nexted once, just short of hearing the words themselves, resulting in the shortest date I've ever been on: thirty seconds or ten minutes, depending on when you stop counting. If I were a NEXT contestant, I would've received two quarters.

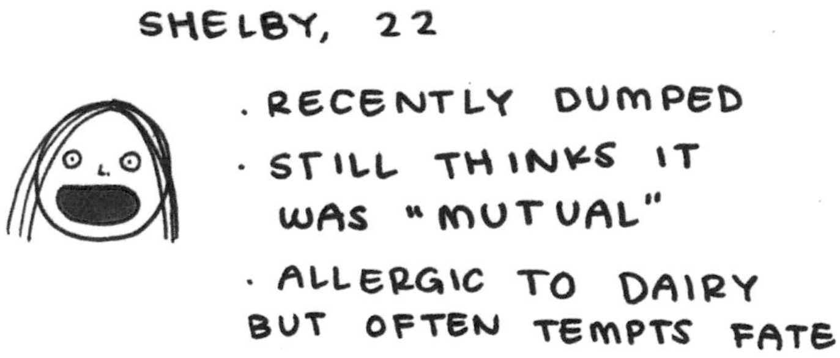
SHELBY, 22
. RECENTLY DUMPED
· STILL THINKS IT WAS "MUTUAL"
· ALLERGIC TO DAIRY BUT OFTEN TEMPTS FATE

It was my first date "back on the market" after "mutually" breaking up with my "first love" (he sucked). I set the date up with "Thane," someone on Tinder who seemed artsy and mundane. I anticipated getting anxiously overcaffeinated and oversharing when the conversation I was desperately fueling like a fire on the cusp of going out lulled, even a bit, and then happily heading home alone.

I arrived first to the coffee shop. It was summer in NYC so I grabbed a seat outside with my "we don't sell iced coffee it's cold brew" that I regretted buying before my date arrived.

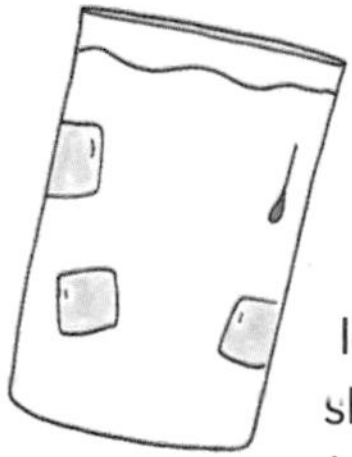

Soon enough I saw a beige blob approaching. The boy himself.

We shook hands, perfunctorily. He put his backpack down by my feet and went inside to get coffee. He returned seconds later, explaining he'd left his wallet, which was inside the backpack. Curiously, he then slung the entire backpack over his (very) narrow shoulders and ventured back inside.

Two minutes passed.

Five minutes passed, my "cold brew" sweating in the sun.

A nervous poop, perhaps? I made a silent blessing for his digestive tract.

Six minutes.

I am an extremely patient person and also loathe moving. I would wait forever.

Eight minutes.

One reason it took me so long to grasp what was happening—that Thane had instant-Nexted me, without even the clarifying courtesy of saying "NEXT"—was because it didn't seem possible.

It's not that I am somehow unleavable, immune to the ever-shitty impulses of dudes you've just met on Tinder. It's that I was sitting in front of the only entrance and exit. How *could* he leave without me noticing, logistically?

At the ten-minute mark, I knew. I started laughing, texted him "what in the world is happening" and got no response. He never answered my texts after that and unmatched me on Tinder.

I suppose I'll never have answers: how he got out of the coffee shop, what he was doing in the meantime. If it was to do with oat milk at all. Why he felt entitled to my time, and worse, left me saddled with the horribly mundane mystery of *why* (and how?!) he'd done it.

• • •

I've told this story to many people, right after it happened and in the years since. I find it hilarious because it's absurd. Because it's so clearly *not how dates are supposed to go down*. But mostly I tell it because it's an easy story to tell. He left, it was funny, I have cosmically bad timing, woe is me but not really. The end.

The stories that were harder to turn into comedy were the more mundane ones, so stubbornly frequent that such repetition made them disappear into normalcy. How could I begin to summarize the lengthy history of not-terrible-but-not-great interactions I'd had with men, romantic and not, the roles so many of us are cornered into without even realizing we're playing them?

In investigating this, I realized my own tendency—many of our tendencies—to put men on a pedestal when they get it right. Or, more realistically, when they don't explicitly fuck it up. When he responds to a text within forty-eight hours, or wears a condom with "everyone but you so don't worry," or when he *sort of* stands up for you in front of his friends: we praise them, myself and many women I've known. We praised the men who didn't leave us on a date after thirty seconds as if, somehow, those with basic human decency should be elevated to sainthood.

It's not just that our standards for boys are low. They are. But it's more than that. The world uplifts men when they do something "brave" like "apologizing" for sexual harassment. It's an ethos that is in the very air we breathe, the way we're socialized, advertised to, educated. It took a long time for me to figure out how to use humor and my cosmically bad timing to turn shitty-but-expected narratives on their heads and, alchemy-like, into content. But hey! You're holding the result: welcome to *Awards for Good Boys*.

CHAPTER 1

BASELINE BRAVERY

BASELINE BRAVERY

OR, THE BAR FOR BOYS IS MARIANA-TRENCH LOW, PLEASE SOMEBODY CALL JAMES CAMERON (DON'T, THOUGH) AND GET HIM TO EXPLORE VIA SUBMERSIBLE

I clearly have a penchant for using pop culture as a way into good-boy phenomena. So here's a really topical example.

At the end of Shakespeare's *The Tempest*—you don't need to know anything about this play to follow—the main dude, a wizard named Prospero, pulls the original Jeb Bush and asks the audience to "please clap" for his final monologue. He's basically like: "None of my art or magic matters without your validation. I need it. It feeds me."

Men, like Prospero, are taught that they deserve to be clapped for, that their very existence and worth depends on it. In part, this is because WE CAN'T STOP CLAPPING FOR THEM. We praise men for rising above the low bar set for them, a cruel irony as they are also the ones deciding where the bar is, like a horrible game of limbo that for branding purposes let's agree to call "white capitalist cisheteropatriarchy."

Prospero was definitely a good boy, which is to say, the good-boy idea isn't new. None of this is new. At all.

• • •

I am an avid chronicler of my own life (both because of my elusive memory and my persistent hunch that someday, among some apocalyptic rubble, someone will find my words and deem them worthy—it's complicated), and even years ago, I wrote frantically in notebooks of my horror at discovering (surprise, you naive nerd) that even the "good boys" would let me down.

For theirs was a quiet misogyny, one that reared its head subtly but reliably—it slipped out like ooze when they were pressed in the wrong way, when I set a boundary or voiced a need or challenged a stance they presented with their particular brand of "I'm exempt from this" authority, reeking with the entitlement that festers from being one of the Patriarchy's Chosen Boys that I mistook foolishly for confidence. I saw but rationalized the endless ways in which they made me small, all while I watched them be praised for doing the least. And I'd often be right there, applauding them, too, sometimes without even realizing.

So, let's give these boys a hand. They need us to clap. *Please clap.*

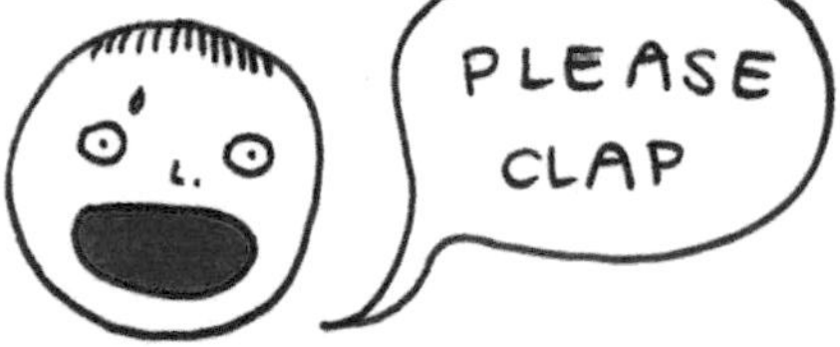
PLEASE
CLAP

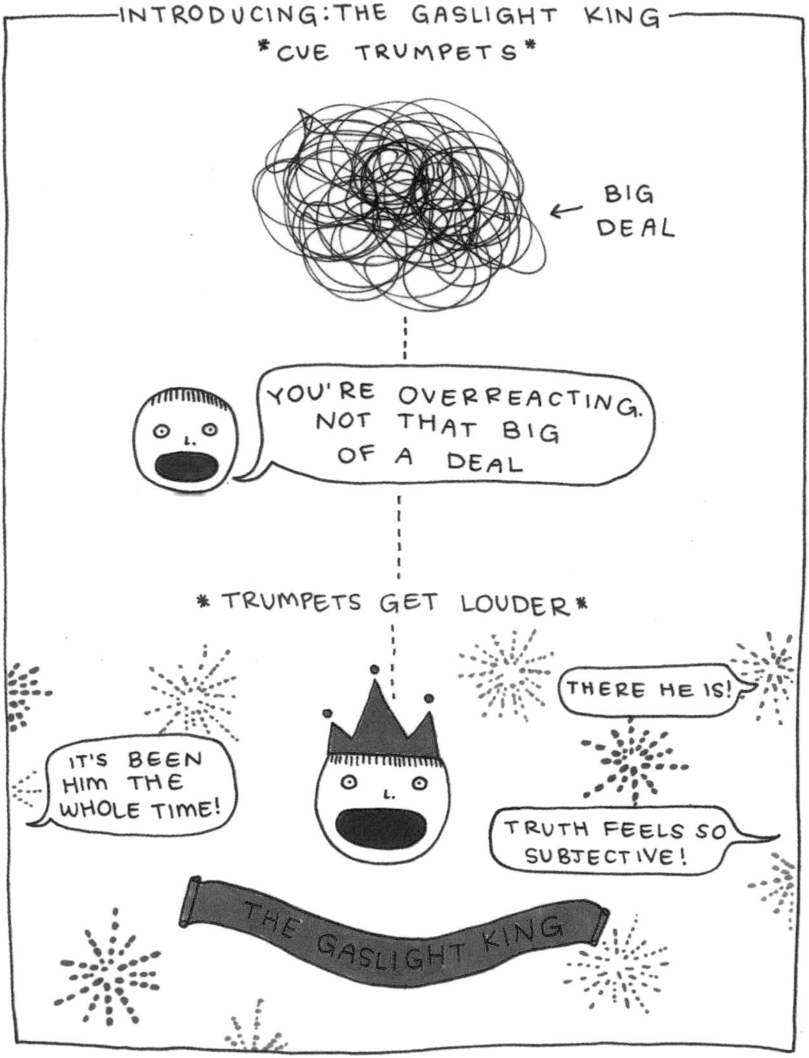
INTRODUCING: THE GASLIGHT KING
CUE TRUMPETS
BIG DEAL
YOU'RE OVERREACTING. NOT THAT BIG OF A DEAL
TRUMPETS GET LOUDER
THERE HE IS!
IT'S BEEN HIM THE WHOLE TIME!
TRUTH FEELS SO SUBJECTIVE!
THE GASLIGHT KING

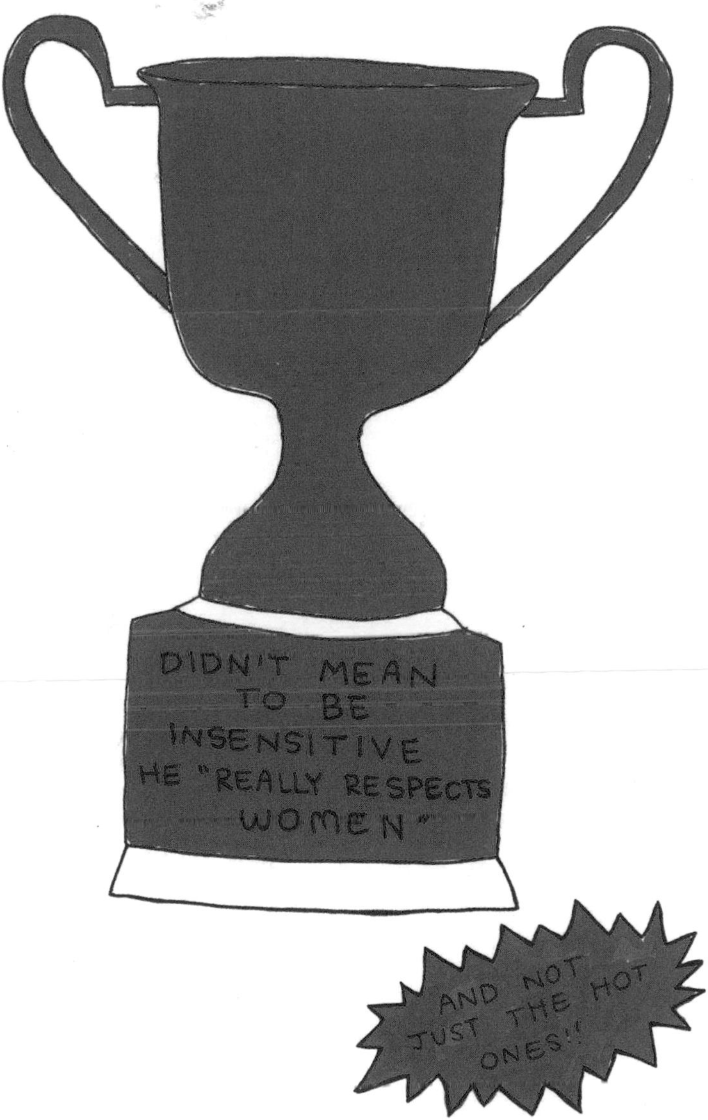
DIDN'T MEAN
TO BE
INSENSITIVE
HE "REALLY RESPECTS
WOMEN"
AND NOT
JUST THE HOT
ONES!!

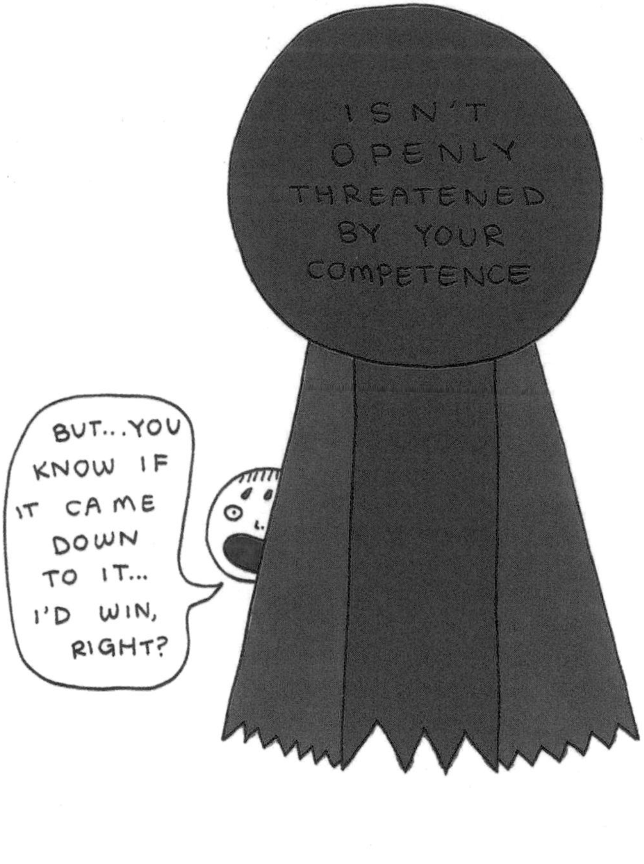
ISN'T OPENLY THREATENED BY YOUR COMPETENCE
BUT...YOU KNOW IF IT CAME DOWN TO IT... I'D WIN, RIGHT?

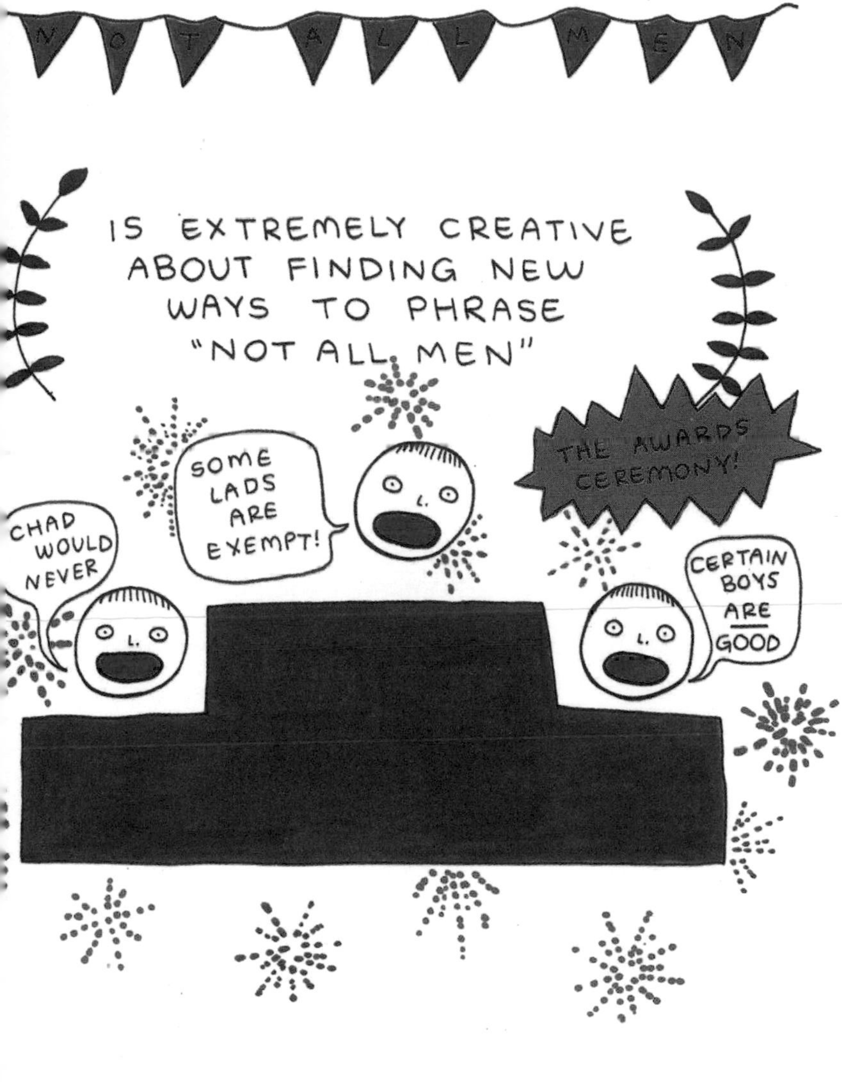
NOT ALL MEN
IS EXTREMELY CREATIVE ABOUT FINDING NEW WAYS TO PHRASE "NOT ALL MEN"
THE AWARDS CEREMONY!
CHAD WOULD NEVER
SOME LADS ARE EXEMPT!
CERTAIN BOYS ARE GOOD

HALL OF "FAME"

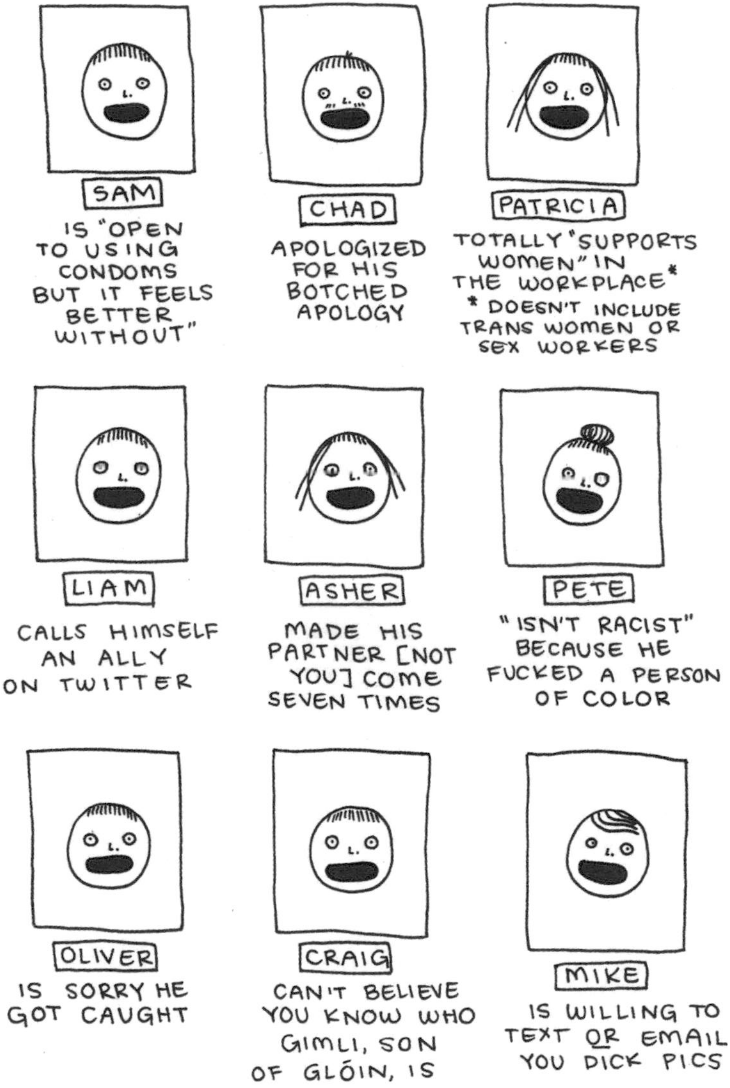
SAM
IS "OPEN TO USING CONDOMS BUT IT FEELS BETTER WITHOUT"
CHAD
APOLOGIZED FOR HIS BOTCHED APOLOGY
PATRICIA
TOTALLY "SUPPORTS WOMEN" IN THE WORKPLACE*
* DOESN'T INCLUDE TRANS WOMEN OR SEX WORKERS
LIAM
CALLS HIMSELF AN ALLY ON TWITTER
ASHER
MADE HIS PARTNER [NOT YOU] COME SEVEN TIMES
PETE
"ISN'T RACIST" BECAUSE HE FUCKED A PERSON OF COLOR
OLIVER
IS SORRY HE GOT CAUGHT
CRAIG
CAN'T BELIEVE YOU KNOW WHO GIMLI, SON OF GLÓIN, IS
MIKE
IS WILLING TO TEXT OR EMAIL YOU DICK PICS

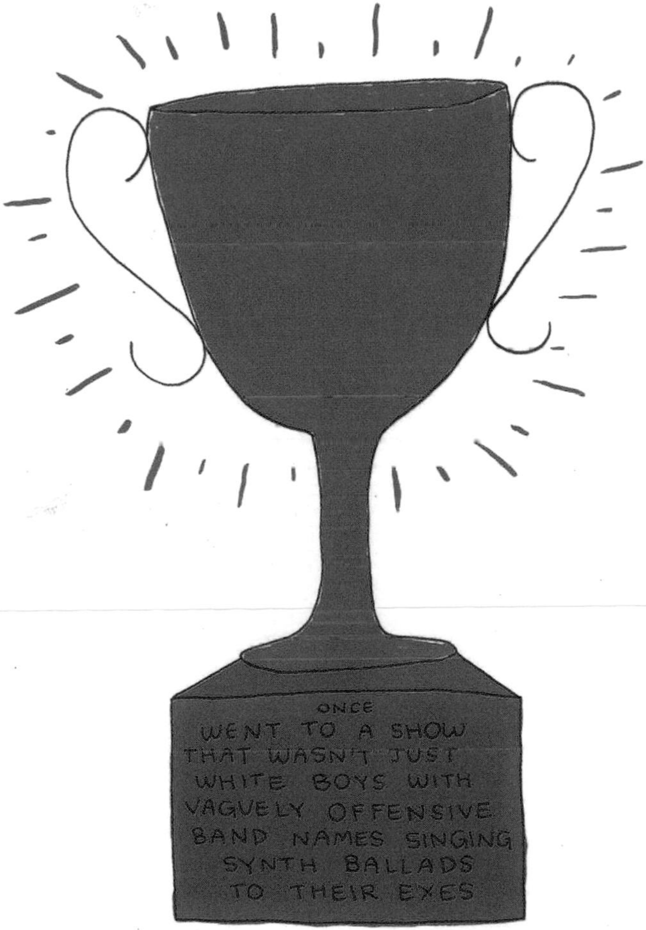
ONCE
WENT TO A SHOW
THAT WASN'T JUST
WHITE BOYS WITH
VAGUELY OFFENSIVE
BAND NAMES SINGING
SYNTH BALLADS
TO THEIR EXES

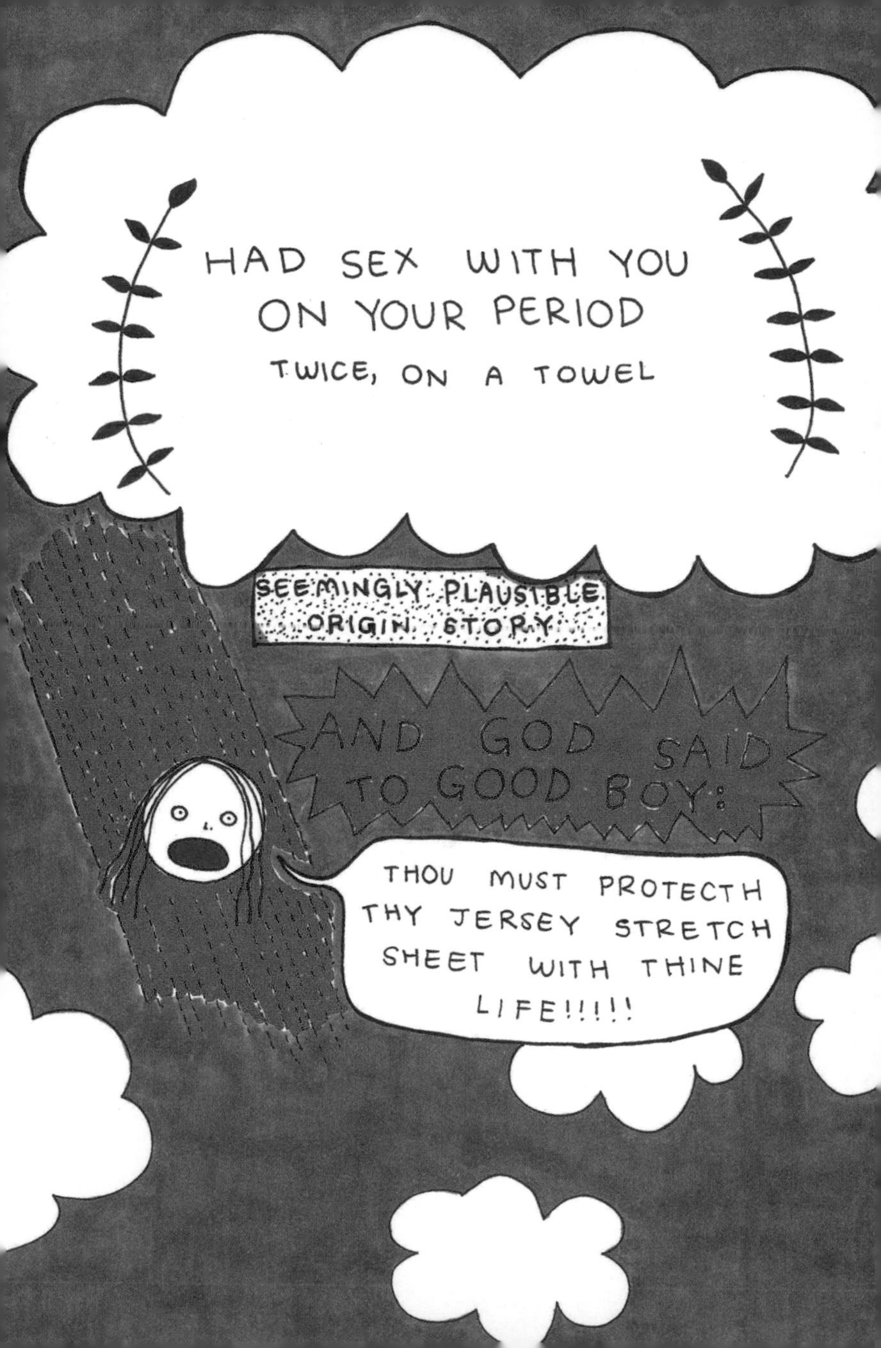
HAD SEX WITH YOU ON YOUR PERIOD
TWICE, ON A TOWEL
SEEMINGLY PLAUSIBLE ORIGIN STORY
AND GOD SAID TO GOOD BOY:
THOU MUST PROTECTH THY JERSEY STRETCH SHEET WITH THINE LIFE!!!!!!

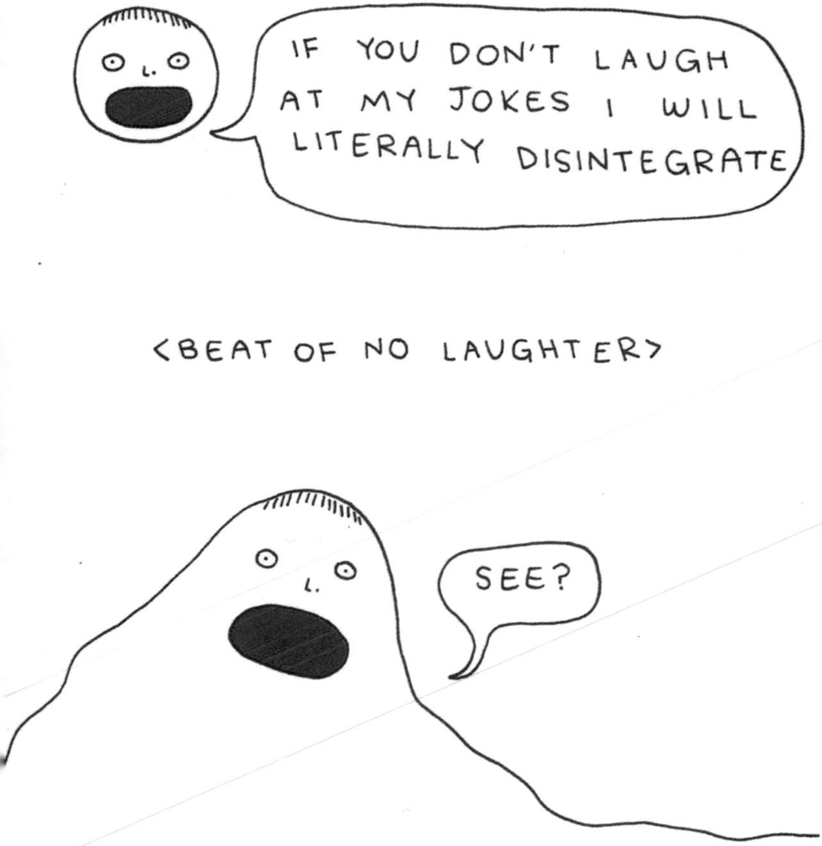
IF YOU DON'T LAUGH AT MY JOKES I WILL LITERALLY DISINTEGRATE
<BEAT OF NO LAUGHTER>
SEE?

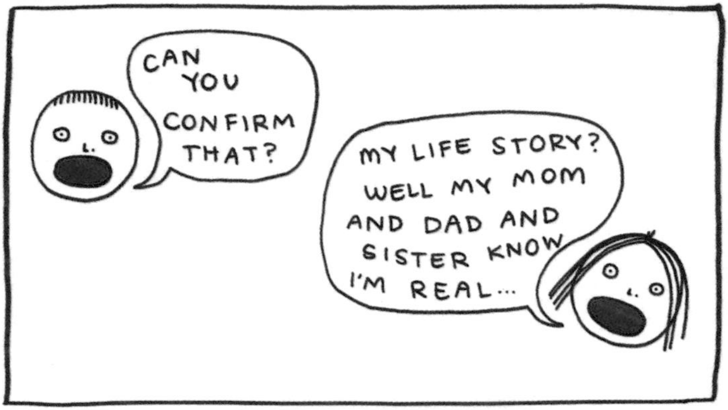
CAN YOU CONFIRM THAT?
MY LIFE STORY? WELL MY MOM AND DAD AND SISTER KNOW I'M REAL...

NEWS TAKES:

LADY CAN'T PROVE LIFE STORY!

WHOM DOES SHE THINK SHE IS??

LIES

BUT ALSO: WHO IS SHE??

BIG FAKE

MEANWHILE

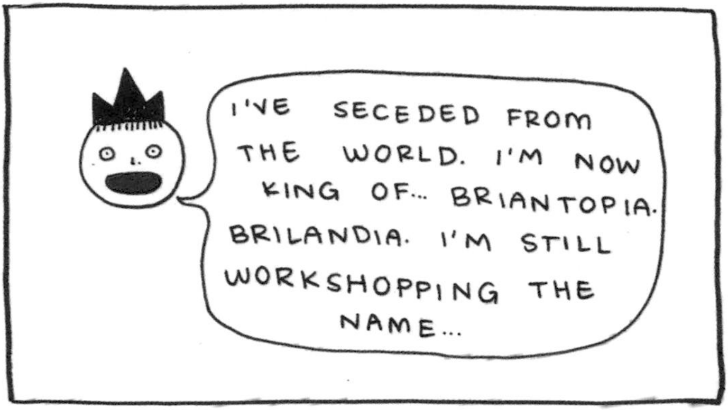
I'VE SECEDED FROM THE WORLD. I'M NOW KING OF... BRIANTOPIA. BRILANDIA. I'M STILL WORKSHOPPING THE NAME...

NEWS TAKES:

HE HAS DONE IT

5 BRIANS TO REPLACE BRIAN

BYE BRIAN: A LOVE LETTER TO BRIAN + HIS LEGACY

223 WAYS YOU CAN BE MORE LIKE BRIAN

WHAT DOES THIS MEAN FOR BRIAN?

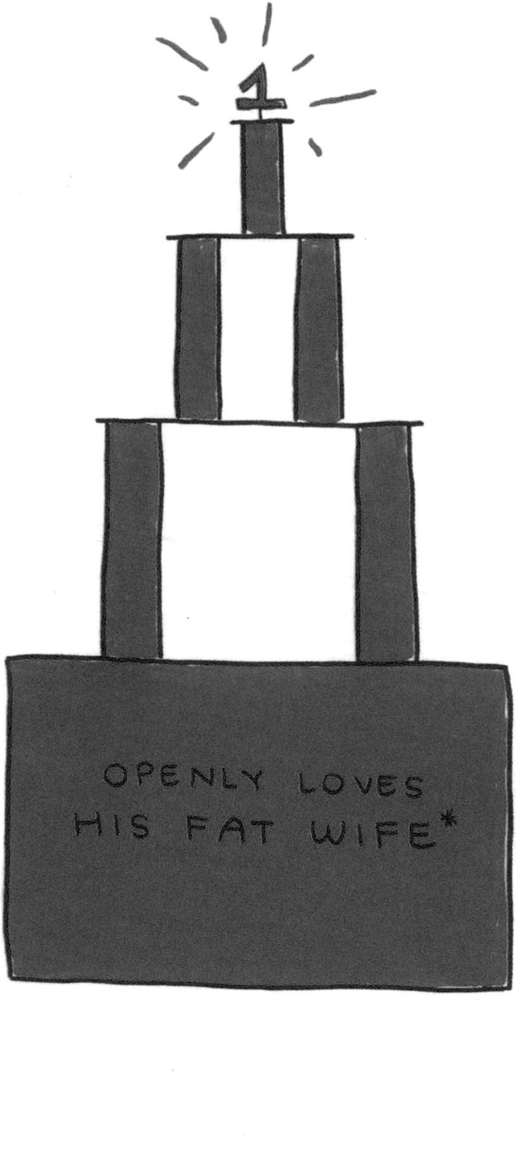
1
OPENLY LOVES
HIS FAT WIFE*

* THIS IS BASED ON A VIRAL INSTAGRAM MOMENT WHEREIN A GOOD BOY WAS PRAISED FOR HIS "HEARTFELT" CAPTION ABOUT HOW BRAVE <u>HE</u> WAS FOR PUBLICLY LOVING HIS FAT WIFE. HE WAS CELEBRATED... BY THOUSANDS... FOR LOVING HIS WIFE. HIS EFFORTS TO BE "SWEET" MERELY REINFORCED THE NARRATIVE HE WAS PRESUMABLY TRYING TO CHALLENGE, FOR HE MADE HIMSELF A HERO FOR NOT BEING FATPHOBIC WHILST MAKING HIS DESIRE/ DESIRING FATNESS SEEM HERCULEAN.

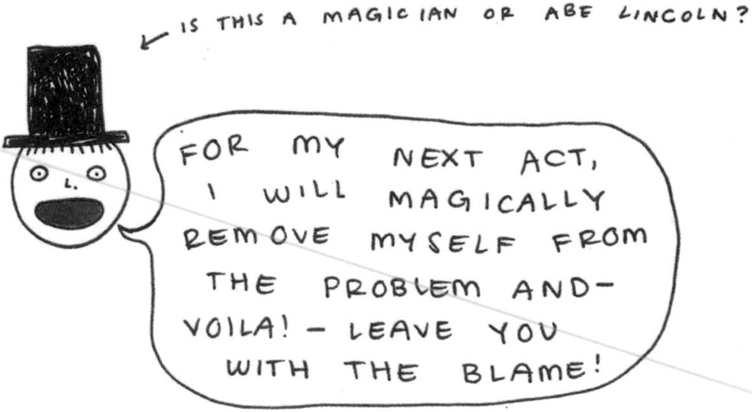
IS THIS A MAGICIAN OR ABE LINCOLN?
FOR MY NEXT ACT, I WILL MAGICALLY REMOVE MYSELF FROM THE PROBLEM AND— VOILA! — LEAVE YOU WITH THE BLAME!

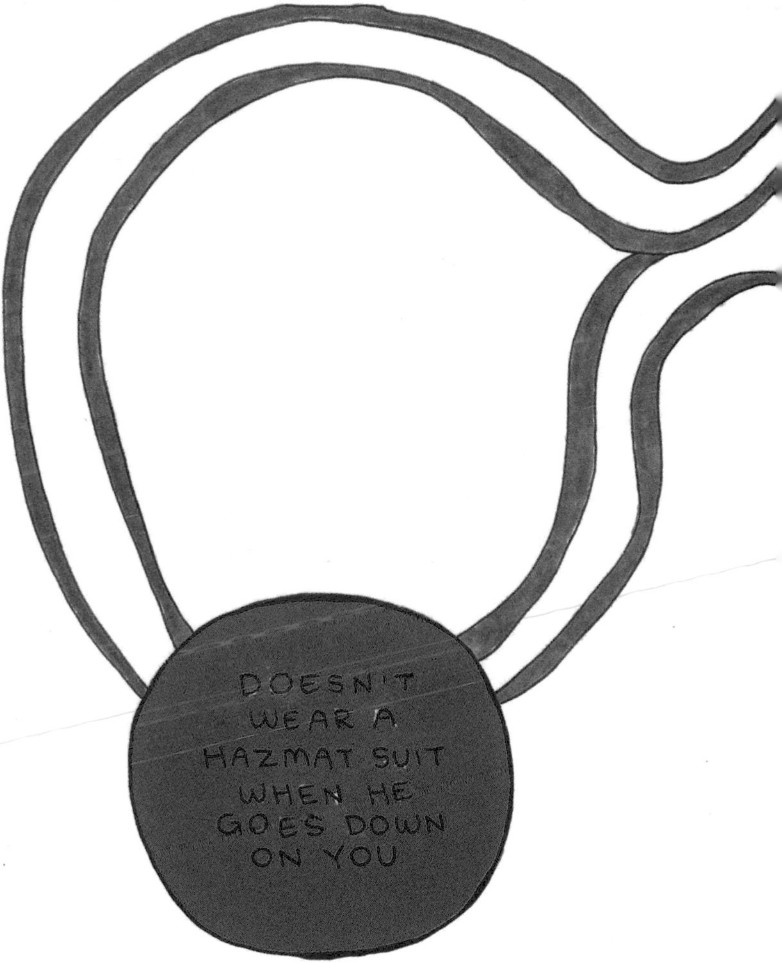
DOESN'T
WEAR A
HAZMAT SUIT
WHEN HE
GOES DOWN
ON YOU

HOW TO DO A GOOD™ AWARDS SHOW

1. HIRE "FEMINIST" DUDE HOST AND LET HIM THROAT CLEAR FOR A WHILE ON META-INDUSTRY SHIT, MUST BE MET WITH APPLAUSE

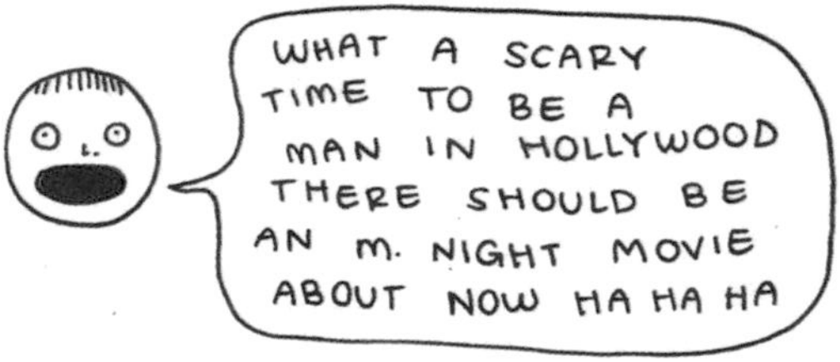
WHAT A SCARY TIME TO BE A MAN IN HOLLYWOOD THERE SHOULD BE AN M. NIGHT MOVIE ABOUT NOW HA HA HA

2. ACADEMY MUST CLARIFY THINGS ARE, IN FACT, CHANGING

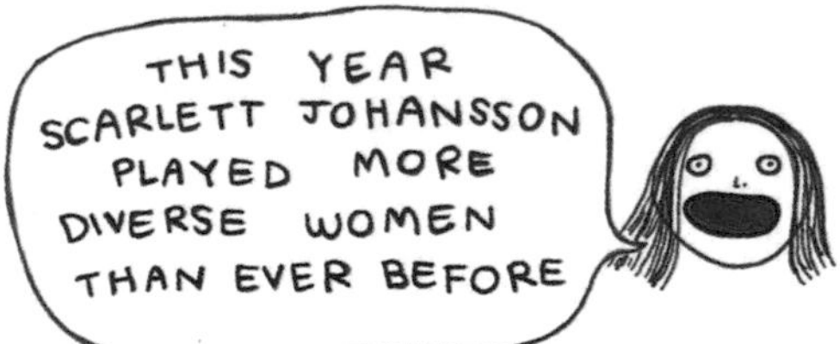
THIS YEAR SCARLETT JOHANSSON PLAYED MORE DIVERSE WOMEN THAN EVER BEFORE

<CLAPS ALL AROUND>

3. SPATTERING OF GLARINGLY APOLITICAL ACCEPTANCE SPEECHES (POLITE APPLAUSE STILL REQUIRED)

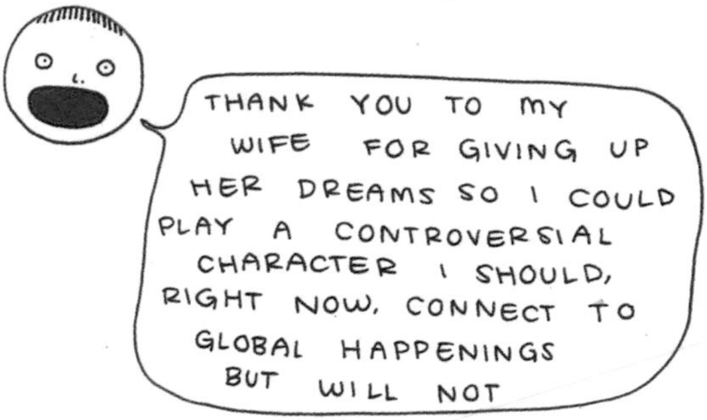
THANK YOU TO MY WIFE FOR GIVING UP HER DREAMS SO I COULD PLAY A CONTROVERSIAL CHARACTER I SHOULD, RIGHT NOW, CONNECT TO GLOBAL HAPPENINGS BUT WILL NOT

4. WHITE LADY CELEB GETS VERKLEMPT ABOUT SOMETHING SHE WAS JUST TAUGHT ABOUT

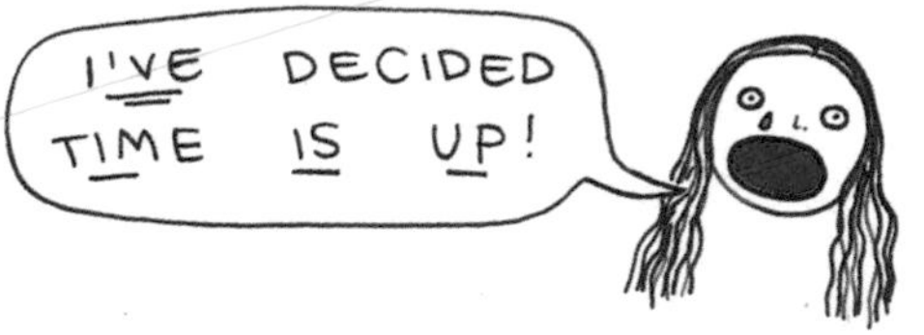
I'VE DECIDED TIME IS UP!

<STANDING OVATION REQUIRED>

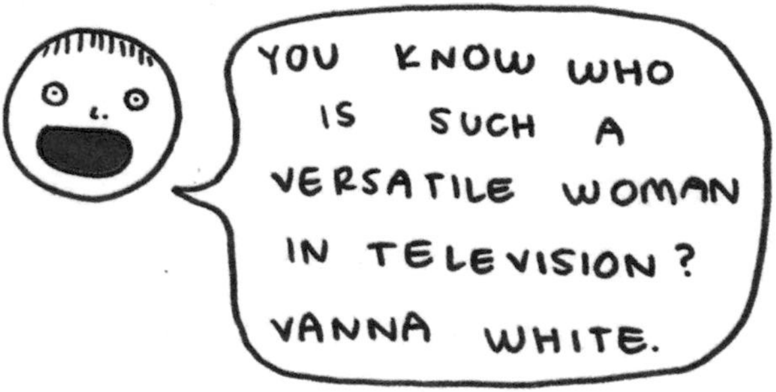
YOU KNOW WHO IS SUCH A VERSATILE WOMAN IN TELEVISION? VANNA WHITE.

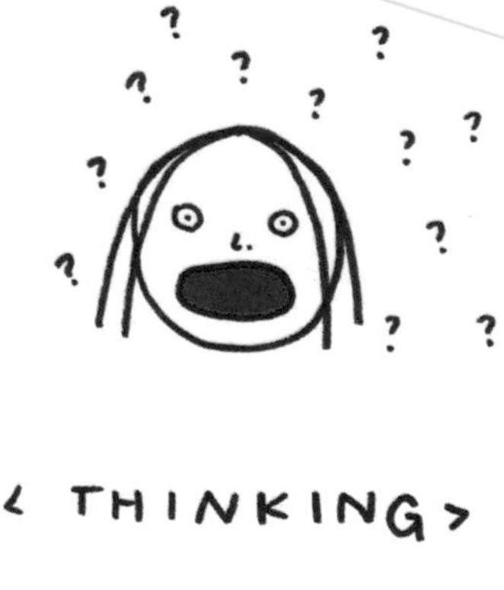
< THINKING >

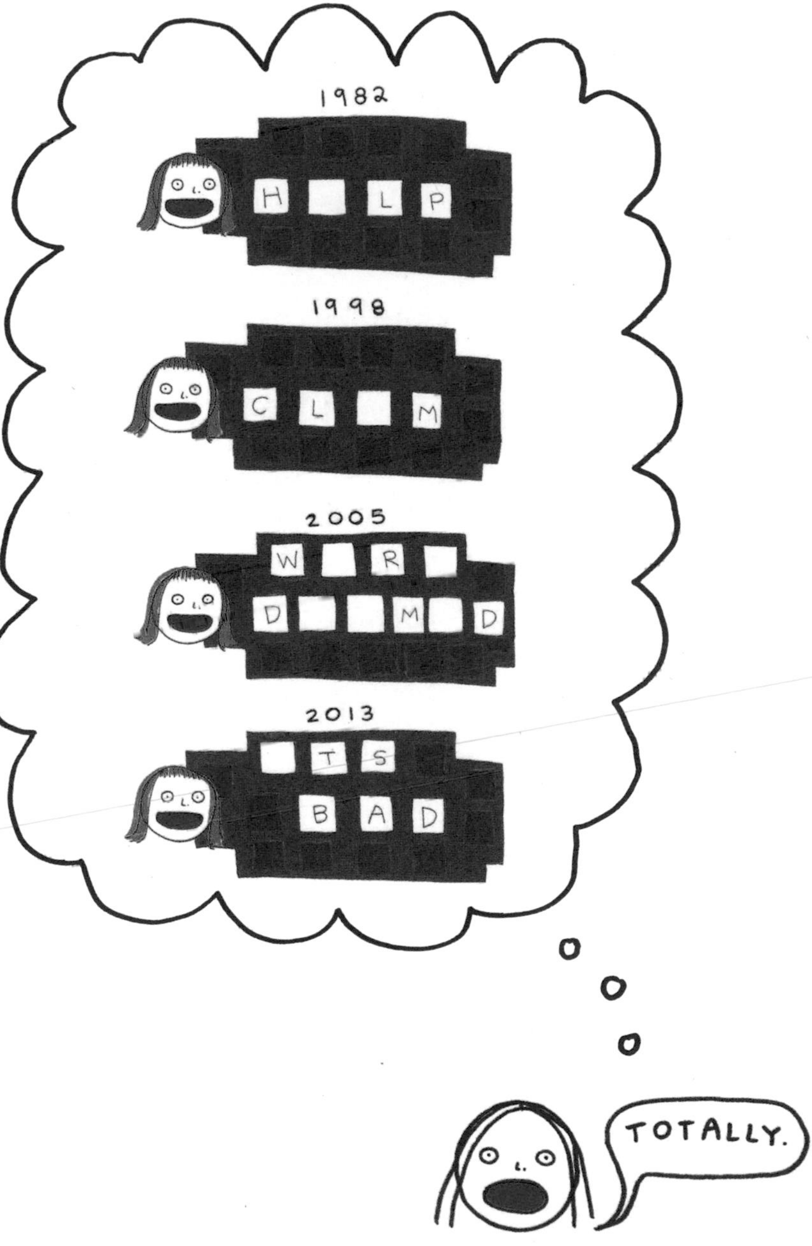
1982
H L P
1998
C L M
2005
W R
D M D
2013
T S
B A D
TOTALLY.

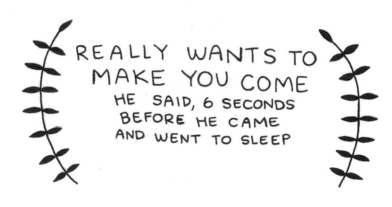

REALLY WANTS TO
MAKE YOU COME
HE SAID, 6 SECONDS
BEFORE HE CAME
AND WENT TO SLEEP

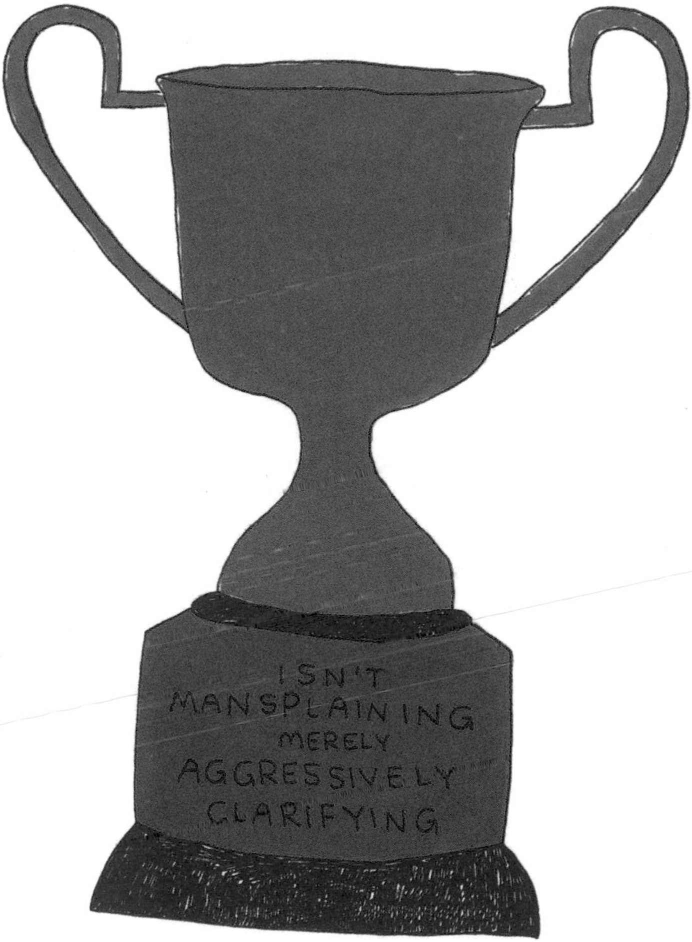
ISN'T
MANSPLAINING
MERELY
AGGRESSIVELY
CLARIFYING

TOOK ACCOUNTABILITY
FOR HIS ACTIONS!

RIGHT AFTER YOU TAUGHT HIM,
AGAIN, WHAT ACCOUNTABILITY MEANS,
PRESENTED A 50-SLIDE POWERPOINT ON
WHY HIS ACTIONS WERE NOT SO
GOOD, PATIENTLY ENDURED
HIS DEFENSIVE FLAILING,
BEGRUDGINGLY REASSURED HIM
THAT HE'S STILL A GOOD BOY
AND THEN GINGERLY TUCKED HIS
NOW GELATIN-LIKE EGO INTO
BED FOR ETERNAL REST RIP

CHAPTER 2

THE PERFORMANCE OF GOODNESS

THE PERFORMANCE OF GOODNESS
(OR, HOW TO MAKE PEOPLE THINK YOU GET IT)

I've found a helpful microcosm of goodboydom in a fascinating and bleak Netflix documentary about the CrossFit subculture called *Fittest on Earth*.

Among other scintillating aspects of this world, in which people compete for the title of "Fittest on Earth" (who knows), is the doubt that manifests around what is, to outsiders like me, so clearly an abundance of prototypical "strength."

No moment better illustrates this than when Mat Fraser, one of the so-called fittest people in the world, does badly in one of the rounds of competition (these rounds consist of them pushing their bodies so uncomfortably beyond what should be tolerated that viewers can basically feel their collective ACLs tearing) and has not just a "well, fuck, that was a bad round" reaction but a complete and utter existential crisis. He turns to camera and asks, without a trace of irony, *"Am I fit?"*

"Am I fit?" asks the "fittest man on earth."

This moment is so grim to me. But it's one that I return to because the phrasing illuminates something so clear. Good boys double down on *goodness*, or at least the performance of it, I suspect, because of this very brand of doubt. It's much like whiteness, like our feminism, like our secret self-assurance that our political be-liefs are the *right* ones. So steeped are we in our perceptions of not being Bad People that it can be difficult or nearly impossible to talk to us about why certain behaviors are not so good without getting defensive.

For addressing these perceptions doesn't just isolate a behav-ior but also threatens to unwind our entire ego and throw our self-esteem into question. "Am I good? What if I'm not? Then *who* am I?" (*Am I fit?*)

● ● ●

Perhaps this existential crisis as summed up by the self-doubt and ego-unwinding of *Am I fit?* explains some of the reactions to the @awardsforgoodboys Instagram page I run.

While there are a whole host of reactions that are not even trying to seem good and enter a realm of comic genius that I feel truly blessed to receive (I once got an email that told me I had ruined a boy's ability to look at his dog, named Goodboy, because of my "negative movement"), some come from a place of someone really, really trying to continue *seeming good* while also offering an unsolicited opinion about why SOME LADS ARE EXEMPT.

The urge to seem good while trying to derail me from saying what I find to be extremely obvious, not-that-radical takes is strong, too, among women. My work implicates women like me, cis women, many of whom are straight and white, because of the ways we form ourselves around and in relation to goodboydom.

Whereas men are quick to tell me my work isn't comedy, that I'm ugly, that I'm a waste—the oldest tricks in the book, boys—women would never! No, when they share their hot takes, it's out of an impulse to spare *me* from *myself.* They desperately try to pull me back toward a more digestible (hetero, cis, white) feminism so I can stop pushing boys and kindhearted girls like them away. "How are you going to give a man a hug if you are in a fighting stance?" one memorable message asked. Who *is* this man? Why do you think I want the hug?

Which is perhaps why women react so strongly when I post things that implicate them more blatantly as part of the problem (Taylor Swift takes, for one). Like so many of us, the rest of the time they're happy to scroll right on by the things that hit too close to home and double tap those that confirm: Yup, you've got the right take! Why dive deeper? You've done it! You believe in the right things!

But trying to deepen and expand the conversation can itself become a performance of "getting it." Signaling that you're "doing the work" can fluctuate into delaying introspection in favor of quickly patting yourself on the back for your "activism." It becomes hollow retweets and comments like "We have to do better" and "I can't believe this is still happening. Thank you for sharing this harrowing experience of trauma *I'll* never have to experience" before you can blink. And what does this do but add yet another layer to the largely digital performance of publicly seeming good? For the most terrible thing that can happen to these good boys and girls is, apparently, to be caught in the web of that ego-dislodging existential question: *Am I fit (good)?*

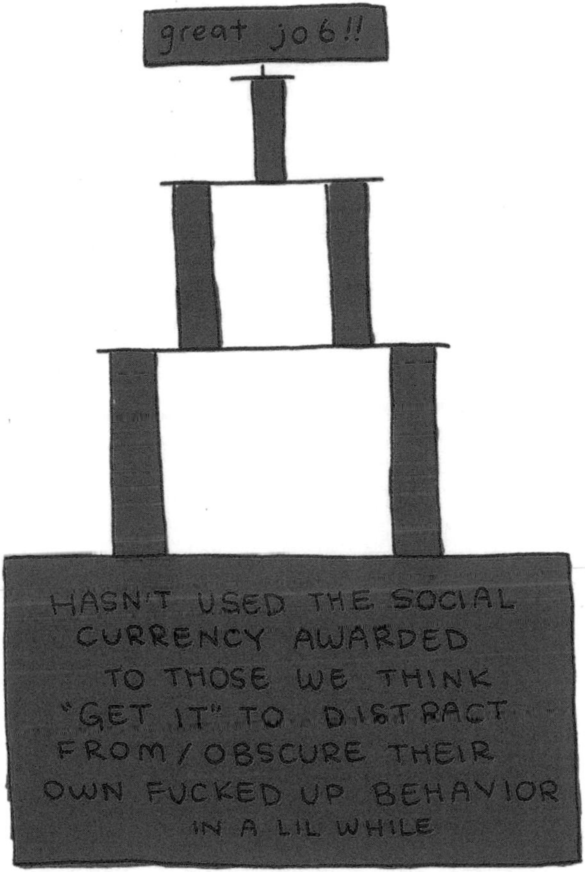
great job!!
HASN'T USED THE SOCIAL CURRENCY AWARDED TO THOSE WE THINK "GET IT" TO DISTRACT FROM/OBSCURE THEIR OWN FUCKED UP BEHAVIOR IN A LIL WHILE

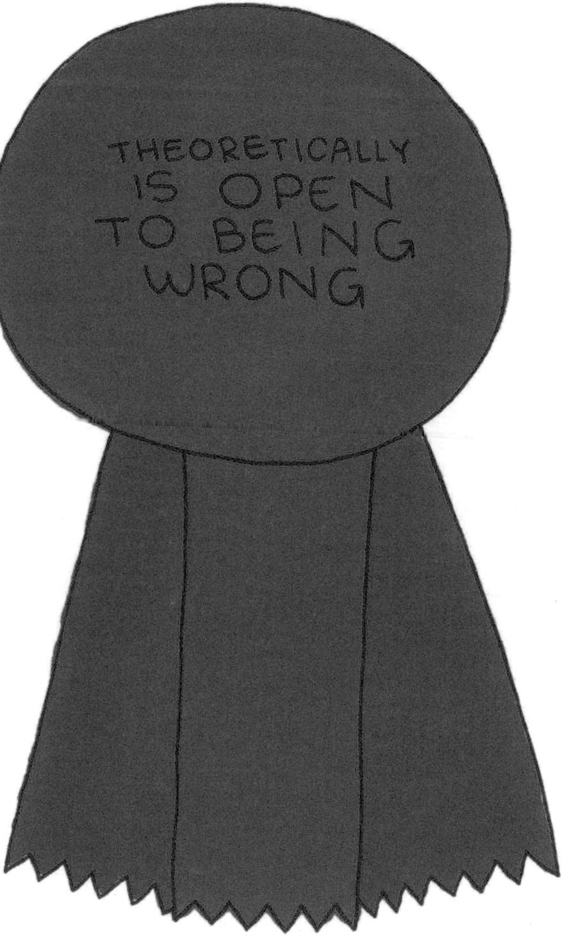
THEORETICALLY IS OPEN TO BEING WRONG

HE'S A FEMINIST! RIGHT UP UNTIL...

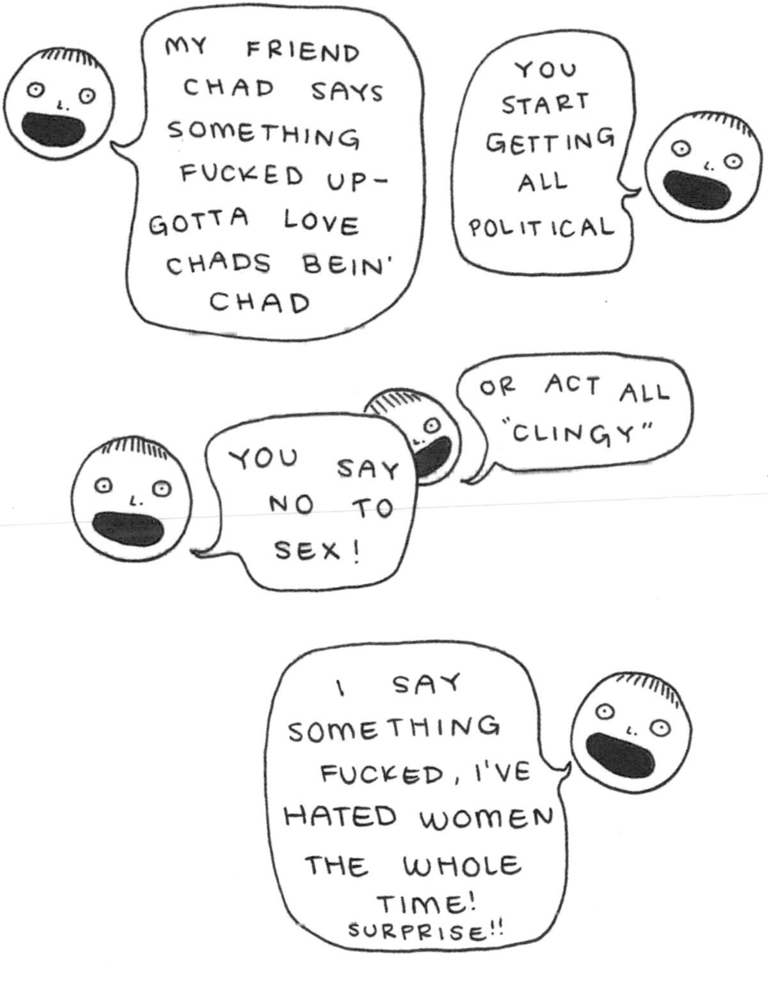
MY FRIEND CHAD SAYS SOMETHING FUCKED UP- GOTTA LOVE CHADS BEIN' CHAD
YOU START GETTING ALL POLITICAL
YOU SAY NO TO SEX!
OR ACT ALL "CLINGY"
I SAY SOMETHING FUCKED, I'VE HATED WOMEN THE WHOLE TIME! SURPRISE!!

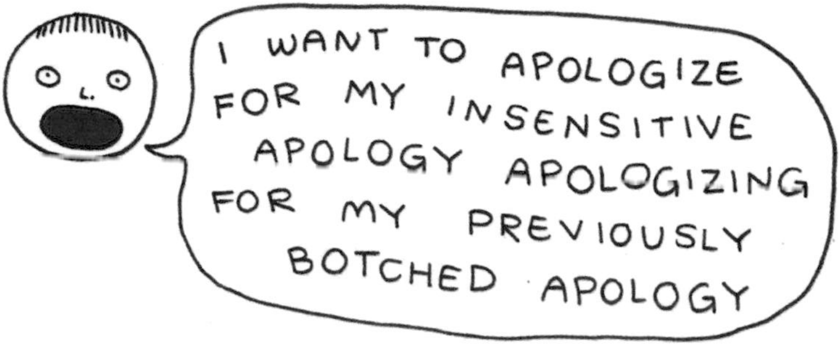
I WANT TO APOLOGIZE FOR MY INSENSITIVE APOLOGY APOLOGIZING FOR MY PREVIOUSLY BOTCHED APOLOGY

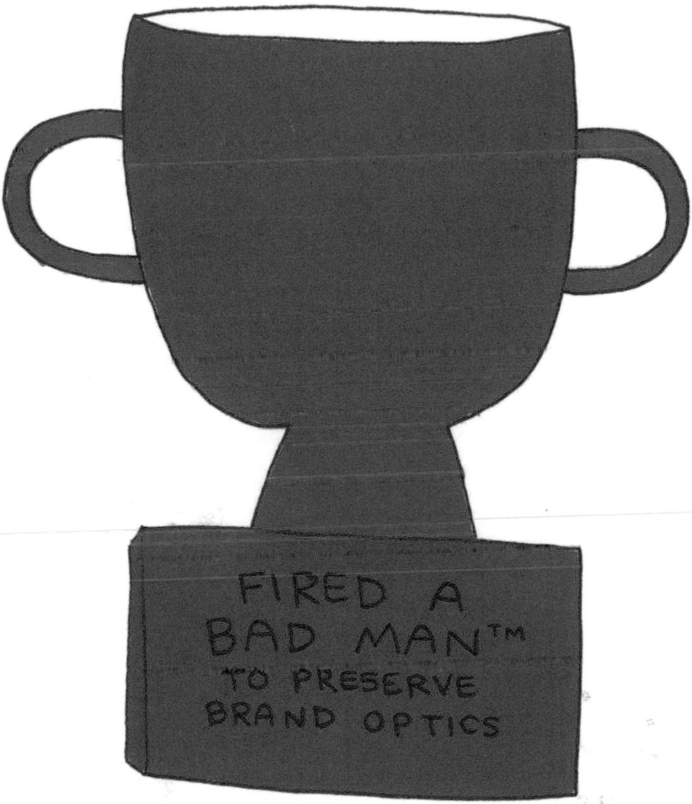
FIRED A
BAD MAN™
TO PRESERVE
BRAND OPTICS

THINKS IT'S OBVIOUSLY
NOT OKAY FOR MEN TO
PHYSICALLY/EMOTIONALLY
ABUSE WOMEN
BUT HIS FRIEND CHAD,
WHO HAS BEEN ACCUSED OF
THOSE THINGS, "IS A
REALLY GOOD GUY AND
DEFINITELY DIDN'T
DO THOSE THINGS"

A VERY NON - OBERLIN REQUEST

I attended Oberlin College, a liberal arts college, the home of many an indie darling and the face of CODDLED LIBERAL POLITICAL CORRECTNESS according to conservative think pieces. I got the "very non-Oberlin request," coincidentally, when I returned to said school for graduation. It came in the humid Ohioan night, just a few hours before I would walk the stage and panic, for the millionth time, about what I could do with an English major after leaving college. (LOTS OF THINGS. WRITING IS GOOD FOR LOTS OF THINGS.)

It was a text from a dude I'd met weeks earlier, in what was a rare instance of me briefly shrugging off the mood of *Is it my depression or chronic illness or social anxiety or general distaste for humans that keeps me indoors like the housecat I was in a past life?* and venturing out to socialize in public. At a party hosted by some very cool Chilean poets, we found we had so much in common. We spoke the same language, he lived in the same building as one of my best friends, and he had also gone to Oberlin, many years before I did. We exchanged numbers because the coincidences were uncanny! I mean, wow!

I didn't hear from him. And then I did.

He texted to ask me out for drinks weeks later. I responded saying YOU'LL NEVER BELIEVE IT I'm not in New York but at our alma mater, my god we should get married can you believe how many coincidences!

And then. And then. I received the "non-Oberlin request."

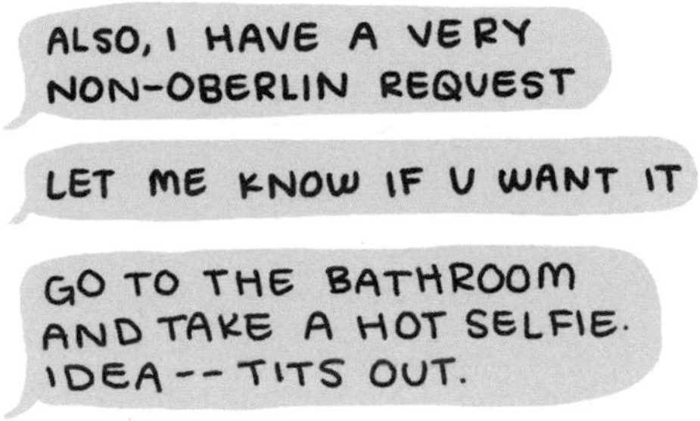
ALSO, I HAVE A VERY NON-OBERLIN REQUEST
LET ME KNOW IF U WANT IT
GO TO THE BATHROOM AND TAKE A HOT SELFIE. IDEA -- TITS OUT.

There is so much to unpack in this, the greatest text I've ever received. It's perfect. It's so beautifully distilled and multilayered in its performativity. Let's break it down. First of all, what does "non-Oberlin" mean?

1. It could be a thematic warning, like, "this next request will have nothing to do with our shared college."

2. It's not that.

3. It's establishing that his request will be contrary to what he knows, and knows I know, Oberlin "stands for."

4. Which is "political correctness" and, resultantly, a very specific set of behaviors deemed acceptable within that framing.

5. So he prefaces his ask with "non-Oberlin" to signal that he's aware of what an Oberlin dude, like him, knows an Oberlin dude should and shouldn't do.

6. And, as a sensitive liberal arts boy who *gets it*, he declares that he is going to defy those expectations but, because he recognizes it, thinks he's found a little loophole.

7. Which, in his mind, conveniently preempts criticism about whatever the request actually is, because he's performing an innate "getting it" so he can seamlessly pull off his really, really well-worded request for nudes without feeling like a "gross guy" for asking a stranger he met one time at a party for a titty pic.

It was like he was presenting the idea to a writers' room or board meeting.

"Now. Hear me out. I'm not saying we should do this but it's just a thought. What if—what if the tits were out?"

"Love it. Love!"

"Big things for Q1."

"Tits out. Great idea. Synergy."

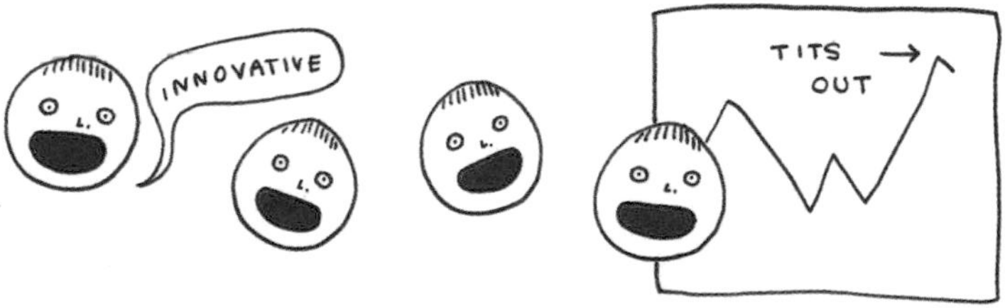
INNOVATIVE
TITS →
OUT

What a good technique! See, he's framing his desires as an idea that I can, but don't have to, entertain. The onus of boob is on me. It's like a hot potato—he's so lovingly passed me the responsibility of sexting. Free the nipple—OR DON'T! It's totally up to you. But if you want to free the nipple and just so happen to take a picture of the freed nipple in the process and want to revel in #bodypositivity and love for yourself, feel free to send it my way.

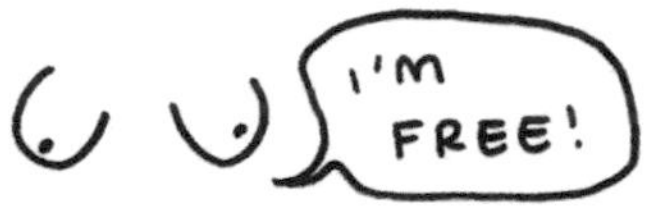
I'M FREE!

I told him "go home you're drunk" and he responded the next morning "Totally. My bad." We never spoke again.

• • •

The non-Oberlin request, though extremely specific, exemplifies a particular brand of performative goodness, which is when a person knows better and weaponizes that awareness to do shitty shit anyway, but more stealthily. A covert attack.

Countless people, mostly good boys and good white women, preface requests they know to be not-okay by draping a cloak of "I GET IT" over their desires so that, if all else fails, at least they can fall back on their good intentions. This deployment of self-awareness is an attempt to excuse behavior one knows doesn't align with the illusion of goodness they project. In a delicate dance, they announce THIS IS VERY UNLIKE ME right before they do something that is, lo and behold, extremely like them.

THIS IS VERY UNLIKE ME!

‹DOES SOMETHING EXTREMELY LIKE HIM›

This trend is different from brands or not-great people performing "goodness," because most of us, hopefully, can spot those pretty quickly. (Lean Cuisine "Having It All," anyone? Bic for Her? Nike? Literally all the brands?) Ha ha ha ha being on the right side of history is profitable and chic now!

But good "liberals," good white people, good boys—we *know* precisely how to perform goodness in a calculated, pretty convincing way, and the result is that it's both harder to suss out what's happening and nearly impossible to address it.

Some of this performed goodness is unavoidable, especially today. It's a living-in-the-internet-age thing. Everything we offer up to the world, no matter how "genuine" to us, is part of a performance that is self-mediated and refracted through the lens of social media—where what you choose to talk about (or, importantly, choose to leave out) makes up a seemingly cohesive whole that must espouse the right messages lest you be CANCELED.

But THAT—the quickness with which we want to cancel or redeem people—is, I think, part of performed goodness, too. It's a way to feel Better Than the Scapegoat Currently Failing, to relegate badness to certain people, rather than look at the intricacies of how we all fail. Because when night falls, even those of us who think we *really* get it, not like those people who pretend to get it, no no we *got* it, are still just looking for titty pics—literal or metaphorical—and asking for them accordingly.

THE GOOD BOY DOGPILE

A PHENOMENON WHEREIN A WAYWARD GOOD BOY GETS CALLED OUT IN THE COMMENTS (OFTEN RIGHTFULLY) AND IS THEN CALLED OUT AGAIN AND AGAIN AND AGAIN AND AGAIN

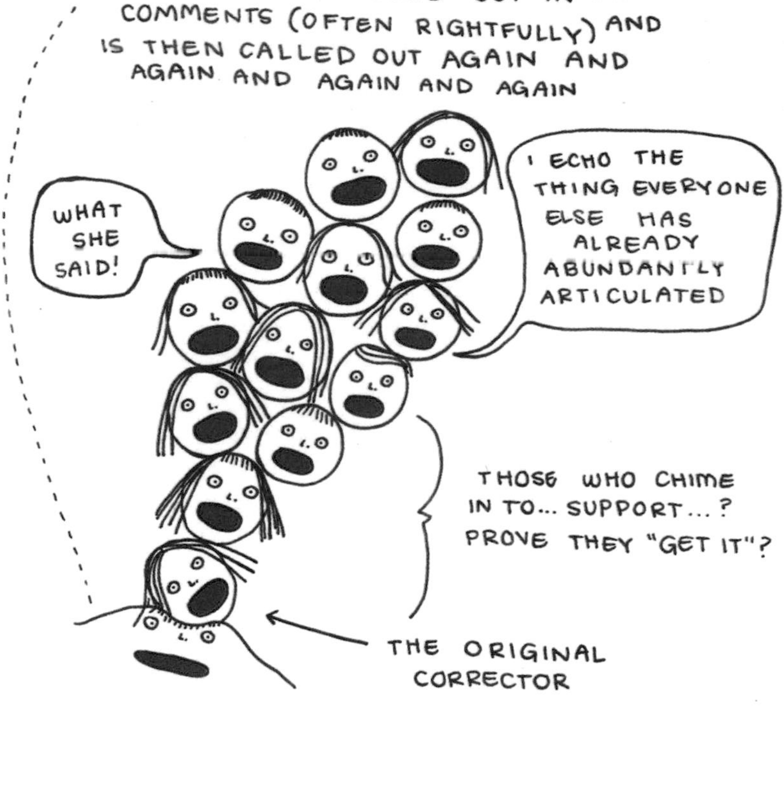

WHAT SHE SAID!
I ECHO THE THING EVERYONE ELSE HAS ALREADY ABUNDANTLY ARTICULATED
THOSE WHO CHIME IN TO... SUPPORT...? PROVE THEY "GET IT"?
THE ORIGINAL CORRECTOR

LIKES HER FEMINISM
LIKE SHE LIKES HER T-SHIRTS
ABOUT FEMINISM:
"CUTE," EASY TO CONSUME
AND TAKE ON + OFF, SIZE
XS BUT "ONE SIZE FITS
MOST," DEF TRANSPHOBIC
(PUSSY POWER!1!!) AND MADE
BY UNDERCOMPENSATED
WOMEN OF COLOR

HELLO EVERYONE, WELCOME TO MY PANEL ON DIVERSITY

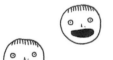

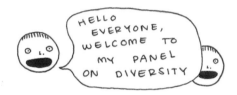

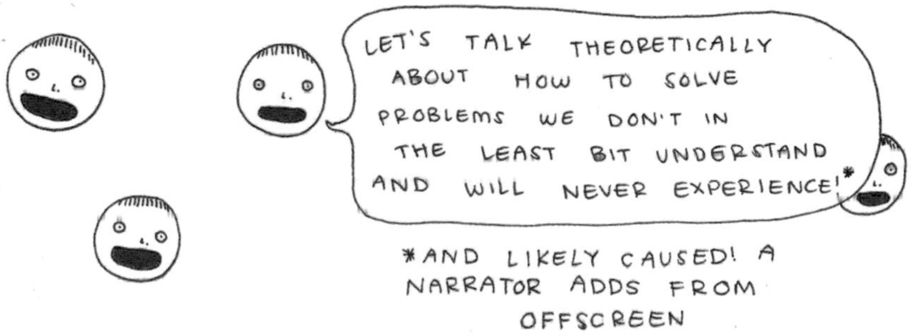
LET'S TALK THEORETICALLY ABOUT HOW TO SOLVE PROBLEMS WE DON'T IN THE LEAST BIT UNDERSTAND AND WILL NEVER EXPERIENCE!*
*AND LIKELY CAUSED! A NARRATOR ADDS FROM OFFSCREEN

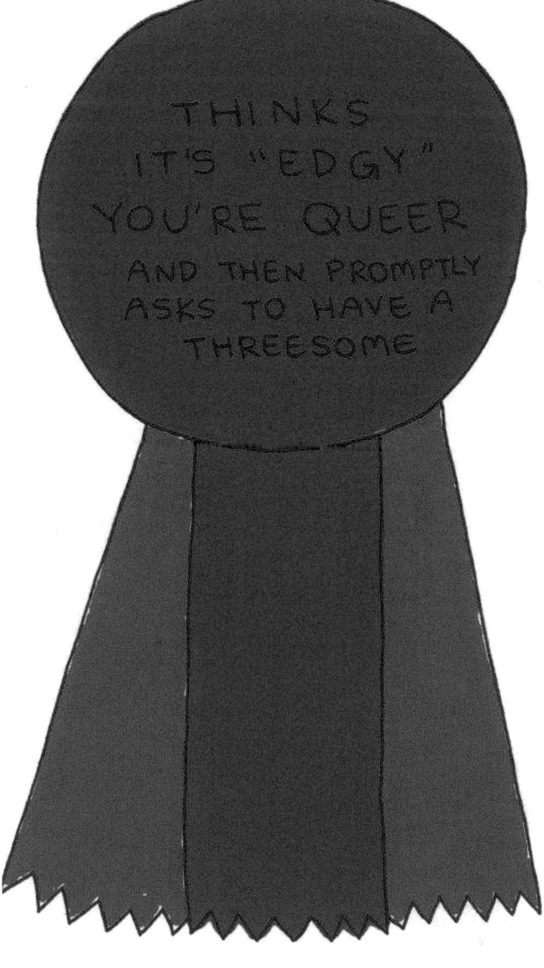
THINKS
IT'S "EDGY"
YOU'RE QUEER
AND THEN PROMPTLY
ASKS TO HAVE A
THREESOME

MINESWEEPER

There was a computer game I loved growing up called *Minesweeper*. It's essentially about avoidance, designated by little red flags. (Spoiler alert: I'm going to make a metaphor out of this.)

In *Minesweeper* you click around as numbers spring up telling you how many "mines" are nearby so you can cover them with flags. If you click on a square that contains a mine, you lose. I didn't really have a strategy for this game (there is, in fact, a strategy), but the point is you tiptoe around mines until you fuck up and set one off, and then you get to see where all the mines have been—hiding in plain sight the whole time—some of which you spotted and carefully sidestepped, but others you never suspected. And then you play again.

To many a dude, it seems, the world today feels much like their own game of *Minesweeper*. They "don't know what they can even say anymore." "The times we're living in" make it hard to find romance, a sentiment that points not to the reality of our trash heap of a world (which, indeed, is wildly unsexy) but to a moment in time where briefly, and selectively, Bad Men are being held vaguely accountable for their systematic abuse of power.

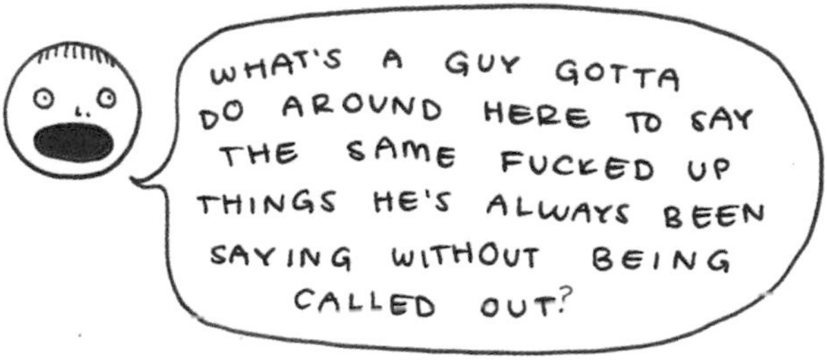
WHAT'S A GUY GOTTA DO AROUND HERE TO SAY THE SAME FUCKED UP THINGS HE'S ALWAYS BEEN SAYING WITHOUT BEING CALLED OUT?

Good boys seem to be trying to do what they've always done, but because of increased scrutiny, feel like they've been sucked into *Minesweeper* in some Cronenberg-esque virtual reality nightmare.

A more apt metaphor is that it's been this way the whole time and they just didn't have to give a fuck before: leaving red flags in their wake and setting off mines, not bothering to look where the shrapnel landed.

Are they really upset at how a "changing" reality that isn't actually changing (much), makes their lives unsexy, or angry that it implicates them in something they fervently believe they are separate from?

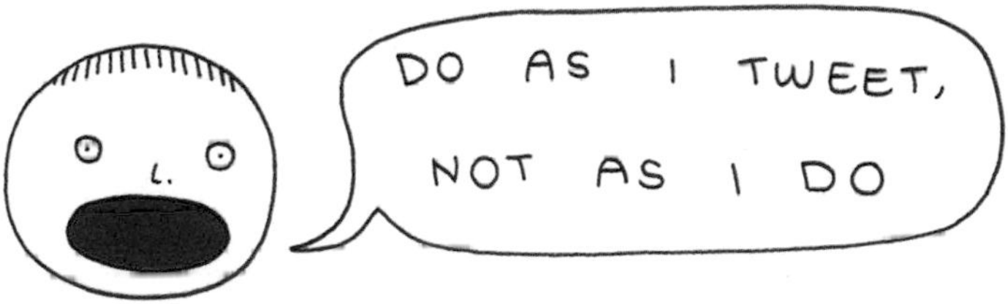
DO AS I TWEET,
NOT AS I DO

THEY'RE GOOD BOYS!
ACCORDING TO THE DATING PROFILES THEY DID, YES, WRITE

JOHN, 27

NONE OF MY EXES WOULD SAY ANYTHING BAD ABOUT ME.

I'M ACTUALLY A REALLY NICE GUY

BRIDGE, 32

"THE BEST BOY." - MY MOM. LOL!

CARL, 22

GENUINELY A NICE GUY WITH NOBLE INTENTIONS

LARS, 28

MARCUS, 29

· ALL AROUND DECENT GUY
· ALLY
· FEMINIST
· I RESPECT WOMEN

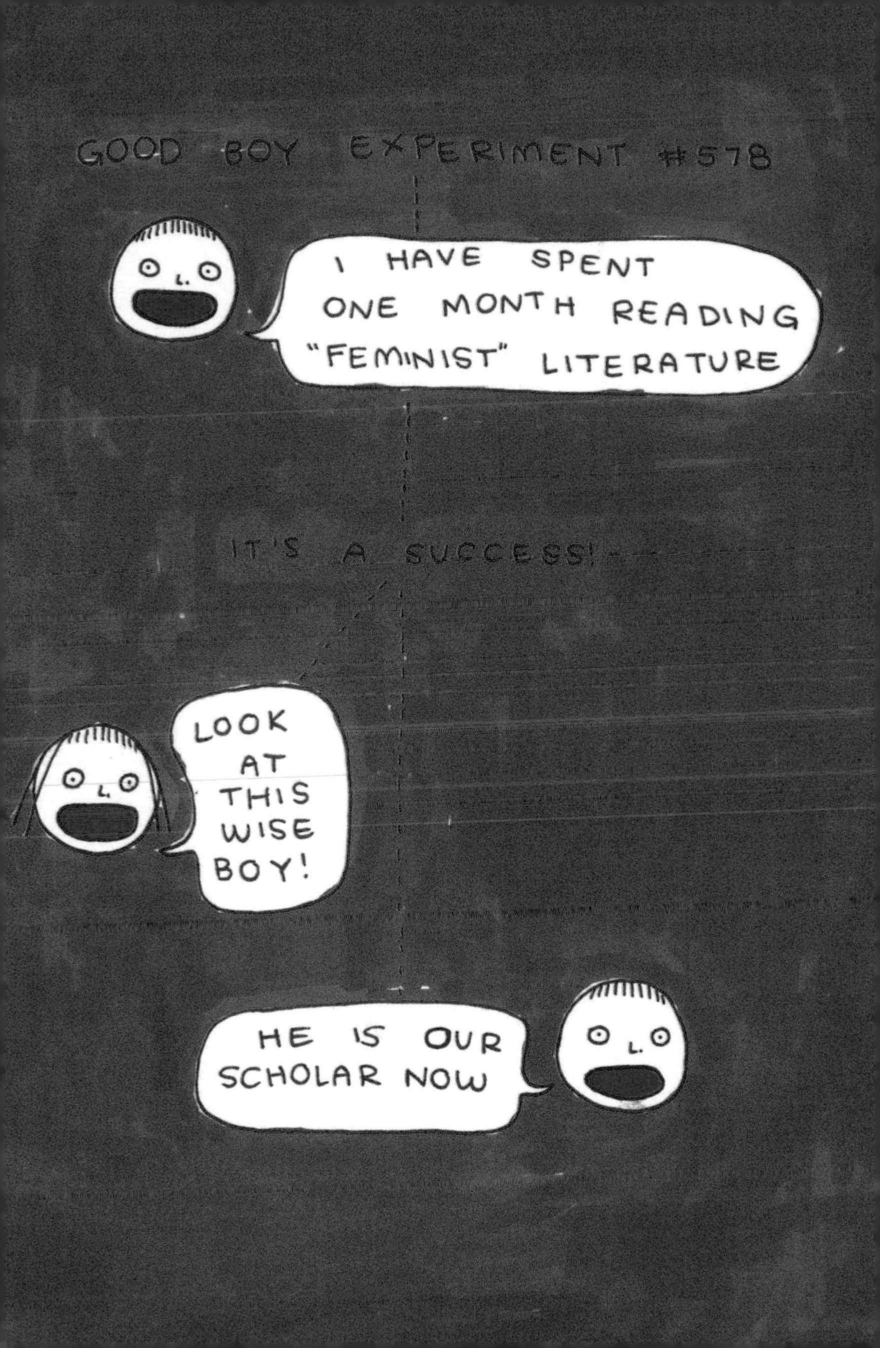
GOOD BOY EXPERIMENT #578
I HAVE SPENT ONE MONTH READING "FEMINIST" LITERATURE
IT'S A SUCCESS!
LOOK AT THIS WISE BOY!
HE IS OUR SCHOLAR NOW

<REMORSEFULLY>

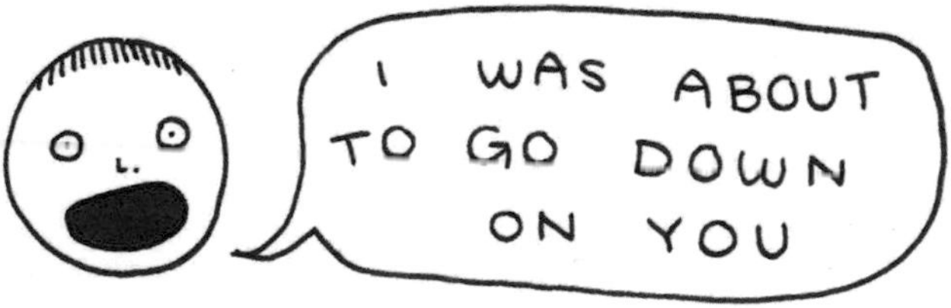
I WAS ABOUT TO GO DOWN ON YOU

SEX TOYS AND THE SCOURGE OF MALE FRAGILITY

I don't even know when I internalized that my sexual pleasure mattered less than men's. That my "stuff" was more difficult, and thus, necessarily secondary. That the sticking-in-and-poking-with-no-concern-for-other-parts-of-the-body was . . . just what conventional, heteronormative sex was.

But good boys are *different*, yeah? They totally care. They'll go so far as to tell you how much they love to make women come. On one occasion a good boy, so proud of his commitment to women's pleasure, told me, "I once made a girl come seven times. That's one of my merit badges for sure," as he was LYING NEXT TO ME NAKED after definitely not making me come seven times.

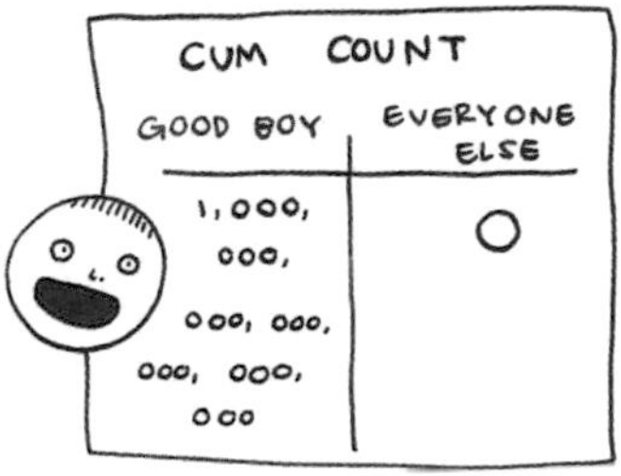
CUM COUNT
GOOD BOY
EVERYONE ELSE
1,000, 000, 000, 000, 000, 000, 000
0

When dealing with good boys, the pressure to assure them they're doing the sex well is strong. (It's very "please clap.") And their awareness of their "goodness" and "not like those other guys"-ness makes them ignorant to the ways they still treat their own pleasure as the default. Their supposed obsession with female pleasure is often just a way to pat themselves on the back that doesn't amount to an action item beyond saying "I *really* did want to make you come."

*　*　*

Let me present you with a case study.

Nothing to me is a clearer example of both fragile masculinity and fragile goodboydom than the terror they've expressed when faced with my vibrator.

"I feel like a human dildo," a dude I was, at that very moment, hooking up with said as I handed him my vibrator, a vital tool in my arsenal for achieving pleasure. Though his was the most articulated version, he expressed something many cis dudes have told me before, when they realized that—alas—their dick wasn't "enough." Which is not what it is about, at all, but that seems to be the easiest conclusion for them to arrive at. "You mean . . . sticking my appendage . . . in the hole . . . with no touching anywhere else . . . your clit being treated like the lost city of Atlantis, mythic and remembered for its glory but submerged too deep to find, ever . . . won't make you come?"

A human dildo. Ah, yes. Asking you to use this tool to help me come (because, surprise, most people with vaginas need more than just penetration) suddenly relegated *him* to feeling like a tool. Fascinating.

"It's very . . . troll in the dungeon," one dude said about my Hitachi, referencing a specific scene in *Harry Potter* where the kids beat up a troll with a clublike weapon that doesn't *not* look like a vibrator. It is *very* troll in the dungeon.

"I don't know, it's just . . . less intimate with a machine involved," another said. ROBOTS ARE COMING FOR OUR JOBS! (I really think this was an automation take.) I wanted to understand. But all I could think about was: if cis men needed vibrators to come, the world would be humming all the goddamn time. Maybe it would even explain one of my favorite conspiracy theories, "The Hum."*

* THE HUM IS A MEDIA-REPORTED-ON PHENOMENON (DO A GOOGLE) WHERE SOME - BUT NOT ALL - PEOPLE HAVE REPORTED HEARING A LOW, RUMBLING, PERSISTENT "HUM."

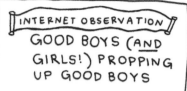

INTERNET OBSERVATION
GOOD BOYS (AND GIRLS!) PROPPING UP GOOD BOYS

1. GOOD BOY GETS CALLED OUT IN COMMENTS FOR A BAD TAKE™

ASSEMBLE! WE MUST PROTECT OUR BOY!

2. SWARM OF COMMENTERS WHO SUPPORT THIS TAKE AND/OR ARE ITCHING FOR A VAGUE REASON TO HATE ON THE SPECTER OF FEMINISM CHIME IN TO GIVE HIM A BOOST

I'VE GOT YOUR BACK, STRANGER

I DON'T HAVE ANY MORE INFORMATION TO MAKE ME BELIEVE HIM OVER HER BUT I TRUST HIM! HECK I'D TRUST HIM WITH MY LIFE!

EVERYONE NEEDS TO CALM DOWN THIS STRANGER IS JUST TRYING TO HAVE A CONVERSATION

SOS

I LIKE THIS TAKE MUCH BETTER THAN THE LADY'S, LOL

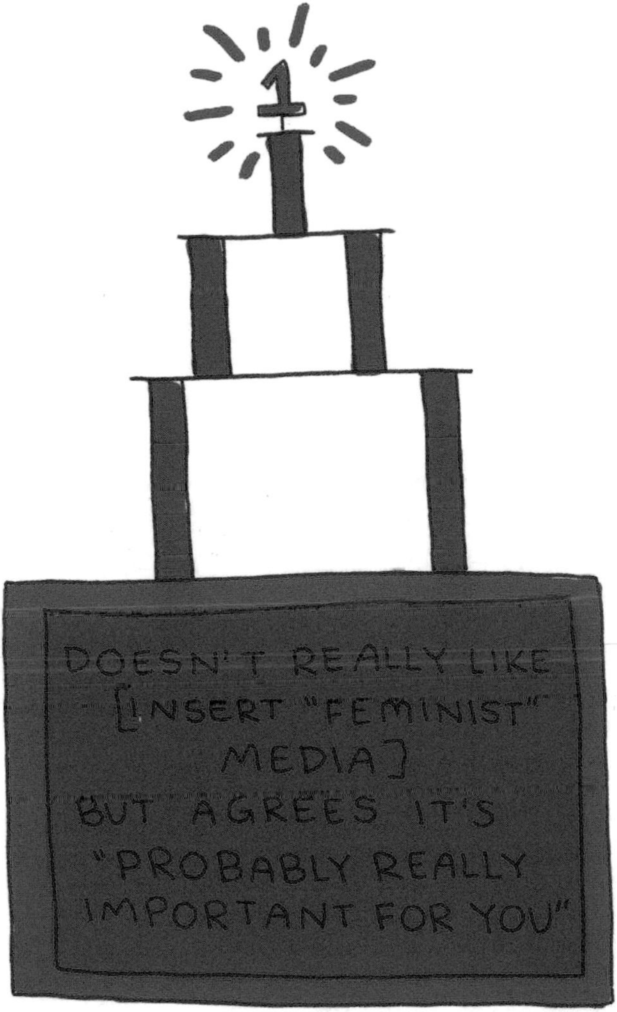
1
DOESN'T REALLY LIKE
[INSERT "FEMINIST"
MEDIA]
BUT AGREES IT'S
"PROBABLY REALLY
IMPORTANT FOR YOU"

FAILED WOMEN'S MARCH SIGNS

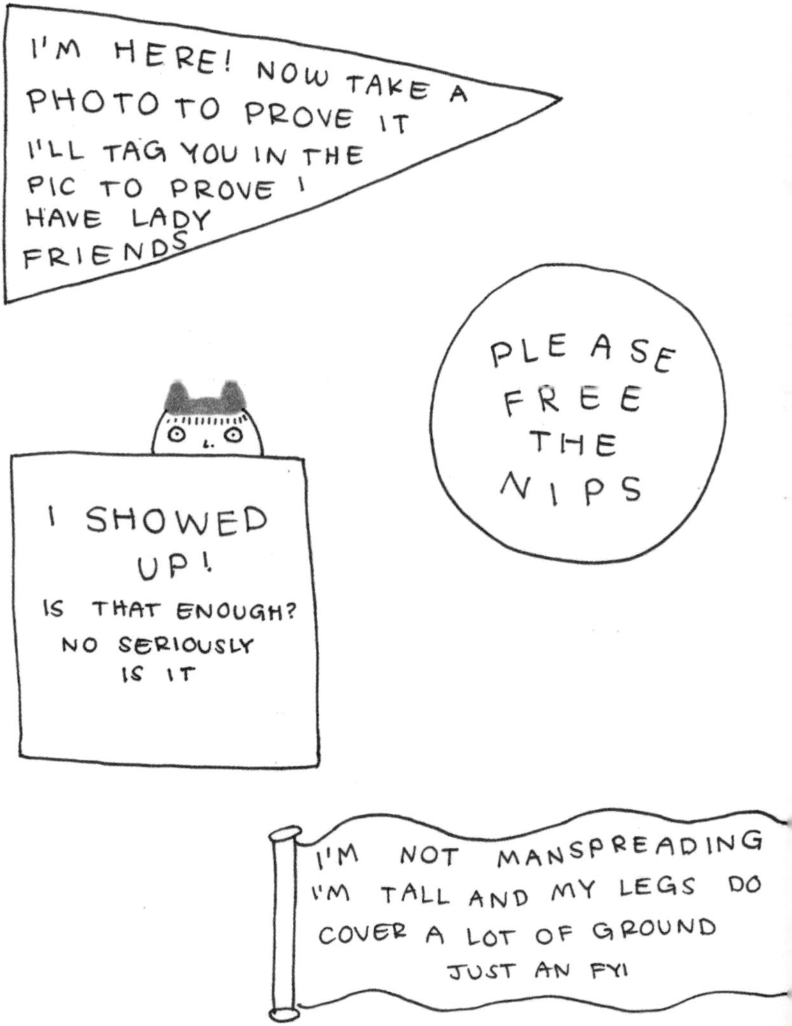
I'M HERE! NOW TAKE A PHOTO TO PROVE IT
I'LL TAG YOU IN THE PIC TO PROVE I HAVE LADY FRIENDS
PLEASE FREE THE NIPS
I SHOWED UP!
IS THAT ENOUGH?
NO SERIOUSLY IS IT
I'M NOT MANSPREADING I'M TALL AND MY LEGS DO COVER A LOT OF GROUND
JUST AN FYI

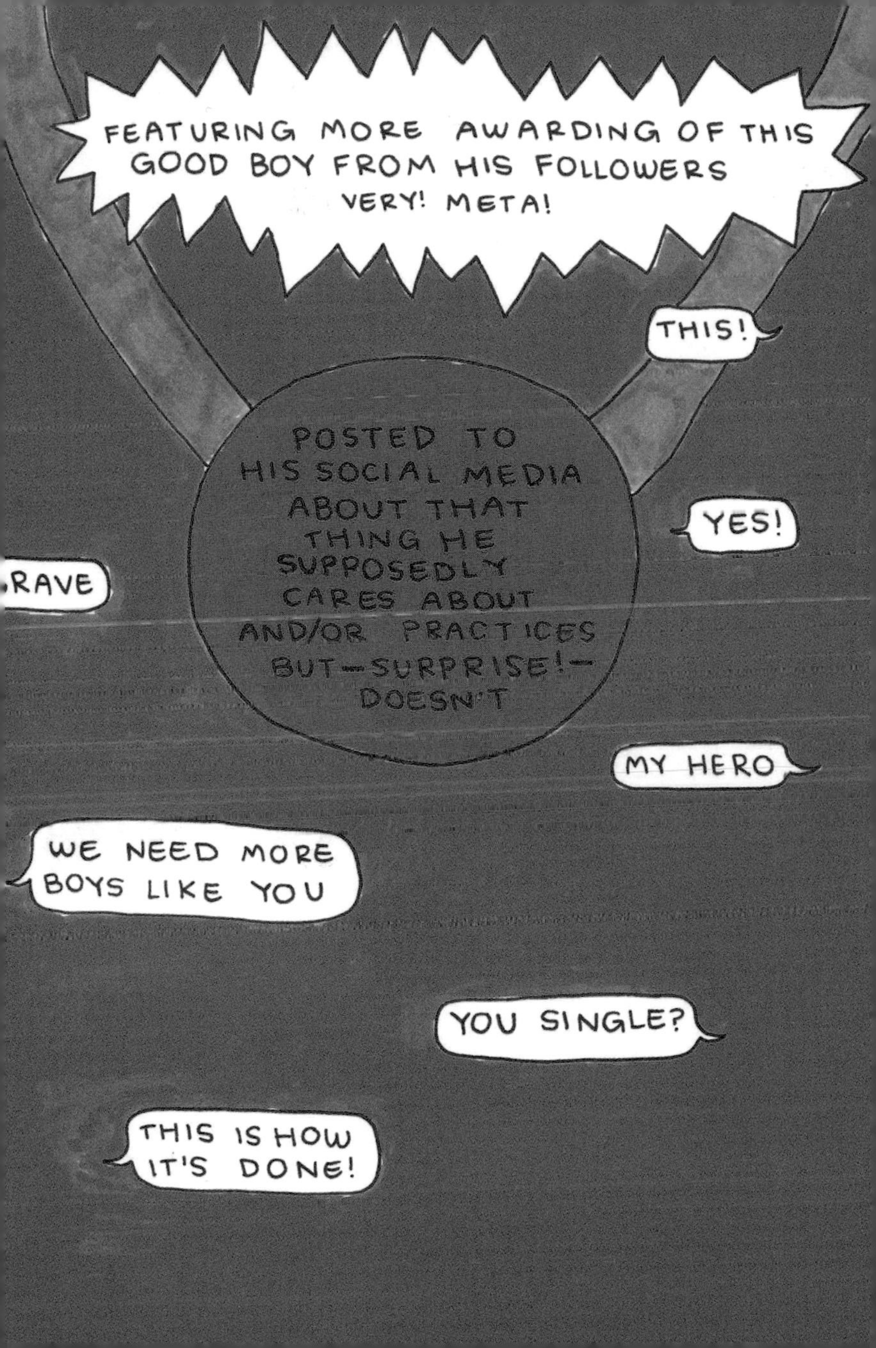
FEATURING MORE AWARDING OF THIS GOOD BOY FROM HIS FOLLOWERS
VERY! META!
THIS!
POSTED TO HIS SOCIAL MEDIA ABOUT THAT THING HE SUPPOSEDLY CARES ABOUT AND/OR PRACTICES BUT—SURPRISE!—DOESN'T
YES!
RAVE
MY HERO
WE NEED MORE BOYS LIKE YOU
YOU SINGLE?
THIS IS HOW IT'S DONE!

IT'S UP TO US GOOD BOYS TO TELL OTHER PEOPLE JUST HOW GOOD WE ARE!
YEAH!
I'M A GOOD BOY!
#ME TOO! FUCK I MEAN #ME AS WELL, ME... ALSO
FFFFF

CHAPTER 3

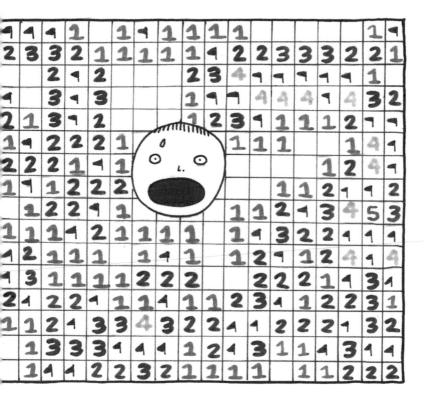

THE SPREAD

THE SPREAD

I've lived in New York for a few years now. One of many fascinating things you can observe in this city if you're paying attention is the subway squish.

The squished person is, of course, squished. Nine point nine times out of ten the squished person, regardless of size, is sitting wedged between two men who are taking up an absurd amount of space. The classic "manspread": the leg spread, which has been justified to me by men with, basically, "What can I say, my dick needs to breathe." But there's also the arm spread, the film gear spread, the HELLO THIS IS MY BACKPACK, THE LARGEST PACK IN THE LAND spread, the bass case(s) spread, the I JUST WENT TO IKEA spread, the I GUESS NOW SEEMS AS GOOD A TIME AS ANY TO WRITE MY NOVEL! spread.

Manspreading, mansplaining, and other portmanteaus that affix "man" to a word to describe an often-invisible-because-it's-so-normalized phenomenon exist in the same nebula of the misogyny multiverse: men making other people feel really small, consciously or unconsciously. Broadly, these terms denote how much space—physical, sonic, virtual—men take up. And, crucially, their ignorance about the size of their own wingspan.

Men have never had to think about how their very existence is part of the spread. That their tone of voice, their body in a room, their name on an email chain can make someone feel small or silenced. To suggest men be more self-aware is—to go with my metaphor—akin to asking them to clip their wings. It's not seen as a reorienting of space-taking-up but as a restriction of freedom, the loss of that which they always had and never earned. For to examine how much space you take up is to reveal that perhaps spaces that seem to have embraced you were receptive only because of the sheer force and magnitude of your occupation, the historical context that yields such spaces to you.

* * *

There's a strange kinship that occurs when you're being squished and you make eye contact with someone else being squished. It's a too-knowing glance shared with a stranger, silently acknowledging that you're both trapped in the orbit of the familiar gravity-mass of men who move through the world as if it is theirs.

That look transcends the horror that is the New York City subway. It's a look I've shared with a coworker in meetings when a man repeats her idea louder or rejects it on the premise that it's too [insert any condescending adjective]. It's a look I've shared with another woman when we were both forced to clap and feign support for an accused sexual assaulter. It's one we share when guys—perhaps ones we love—speak over us or neglect to ask for our opinion and never seem curious about what wasn't said, what they lost, in that silencing.

Good boys are not innocent of the spread, though their version looks different. If anything, it's harder to get good boys to look at how much space they take up, so certain are they that it's just the right amount.

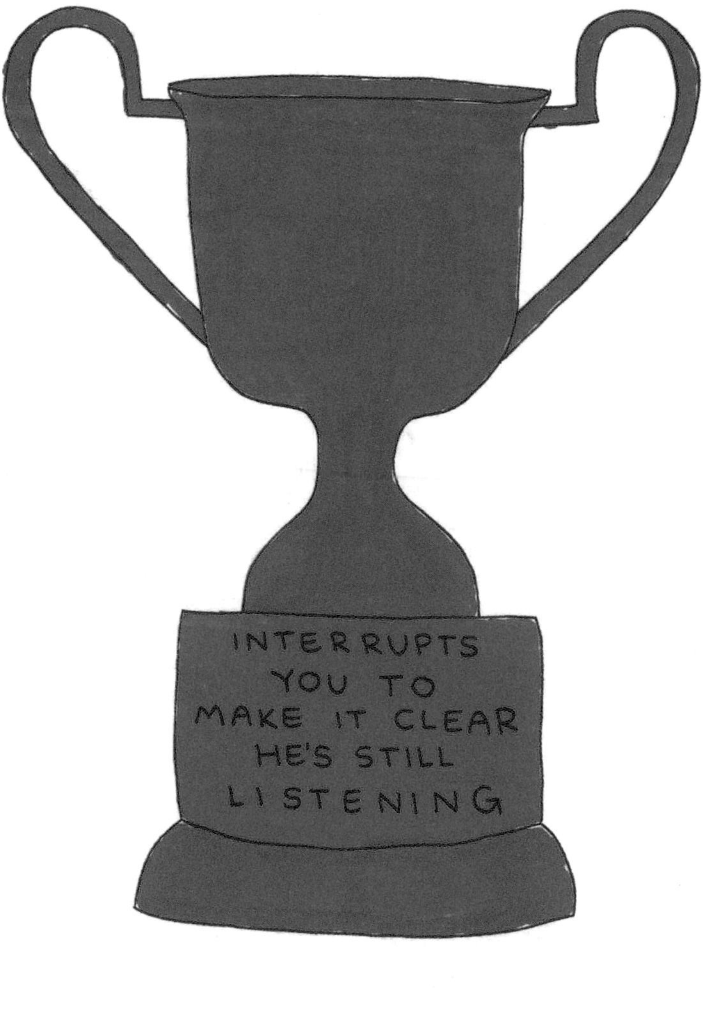
INTERRUPTS
YOU TO
MAKE IT CLEAR
HE'S STILL
LISTENING

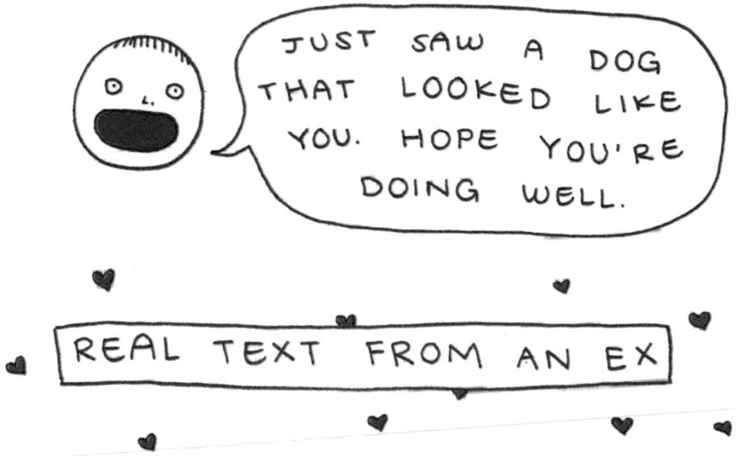
JUST SAW A DOG THAT LOOKED LIKE YOU. HOPE YOU'RE DOING WELL.
REAL TEXT FROM AN EX

<SHOUTS AT UNSMILING PERSON>

SMILE FOR ME!
NOT SMILING

WHAT HE THINKS WILL HAPPEN...?

ANYTHING FOR YOU, HOT ~~STRANGE~~ MAN WITH A REALLY INNOVATIVE ASK! LET'S GET MARRIED?

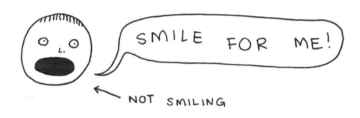

WHAT WILL ACTUALLY
HAPPEN:

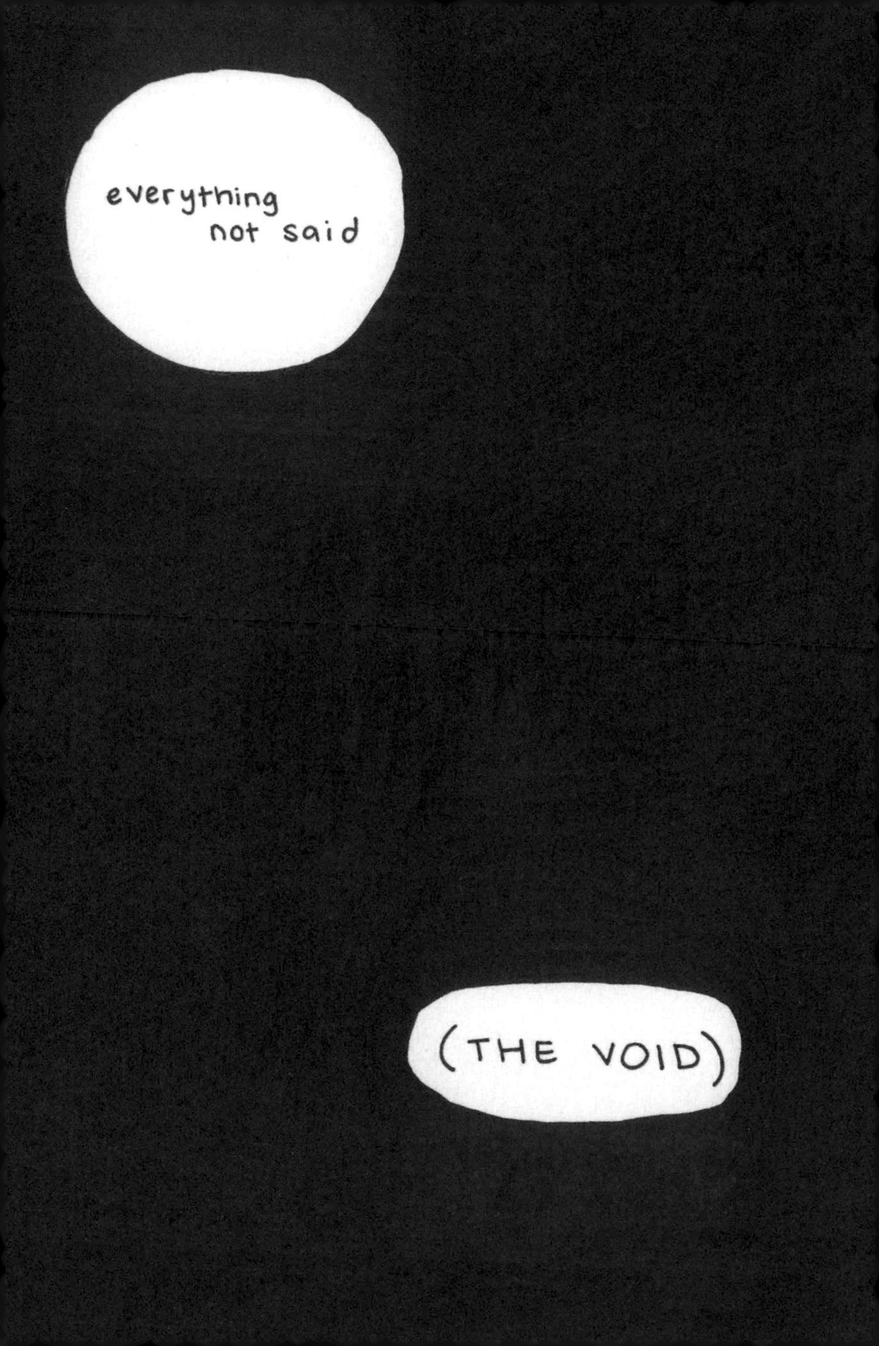
everything not said
(THE VOID)

THE SPREAD:
THREE MANIFESTATIONS

There are three nonphysical aspects of the spread, by my definition. (I'm going to lump phenomena of various degrees of severity
together. I know. It's a lot to handle. *Will* women be able to differ-
entiate them, to know that some are inherently worse than
others? I don't know. We are so bad at nuance. Please help us.)

There's the sonic spread. The most obvious example is street
harassment. But men also occupy and puncture space around
them in more subtle ways: always speaking first in class or in
meetings; interrupting; not leaving space for not-men; talking
over people; undermining the ideas/word choice of others; tone-
policing; being unaware of their own volume.

Then there's the digital spread. To put it mildly, the internet
doesn't give a shit about protecting anyone who isn't a white, cis
man, so the entire web is an inextricable part of their off-line
spread. The most obvious example is unsolicited dick pics. But
also: trolling; doxing (WHOMST IS SURPRISED THAT DUDES USE
THE INTERNET AS A WAY TO EXTEND THE REACH OF THEIR
OFF-LINE HARASSMENT, NOT ME!), the practice of finding and
revealing private information about someone—e.g., their workplace or home address—online; sliding into your DMs after seeing you on Tinder; texting an ex months later "just to say hi" after
she's made it clear she needs space to move on.

And then there's the void. The void is everything not said.
Silence can be extremely loud, when used calculatingly by those

normally holding the mic. The most prominent example is men failing to call out other men for their transgressions. Then there are the legions of famous boys who woefully misuse their platforms and fail to call attention to anything real until asked. More subtle instances include ghosting, making excuses, or not texting back but constantly watching your Instagram stories (this is called "orbiting," I'm told by people younger than me).

There are countless examples of nonphysical ways men over-occupy the space around them.

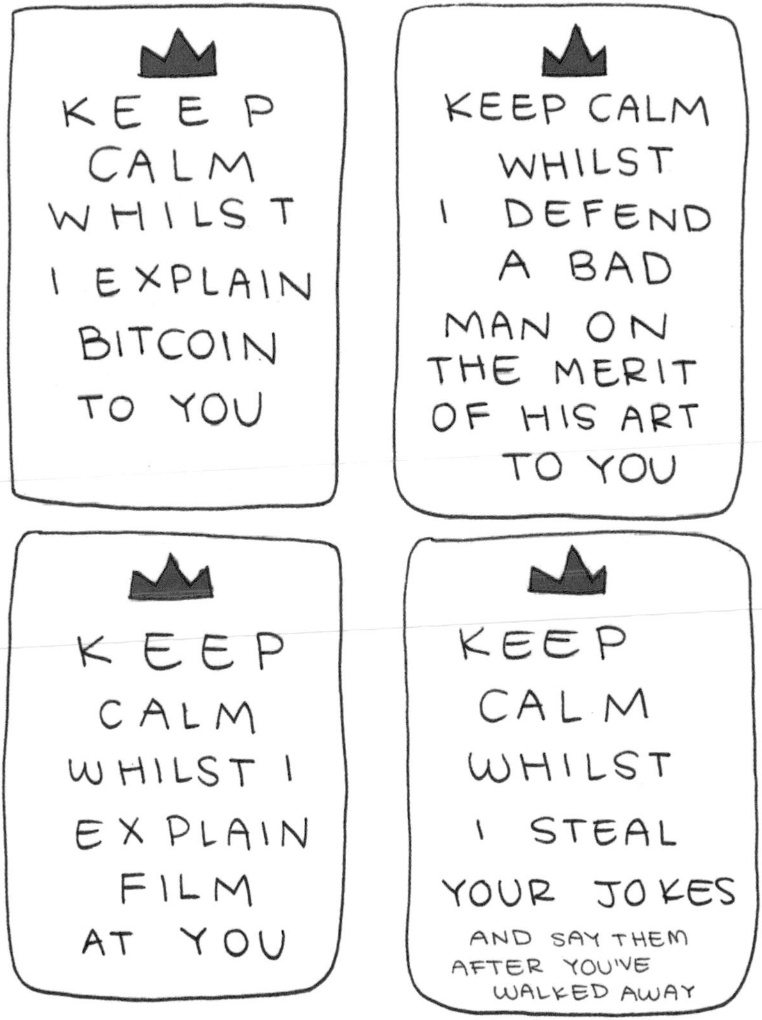
KEEP CALM WHILST I EXPLAIN BITCOIN TO YOU
KEEP CALM WHILST I DEFEND A BAD MAN ON THE MERIT OF HIS ART TO YOU
KEEP CALM WHILST I EXPLAIN FILM AT YOU
KEEP CALM WHILST I STEAL YOUR JOKES
AND SAY THEM AFTER YOU'VE WALKED AWAY

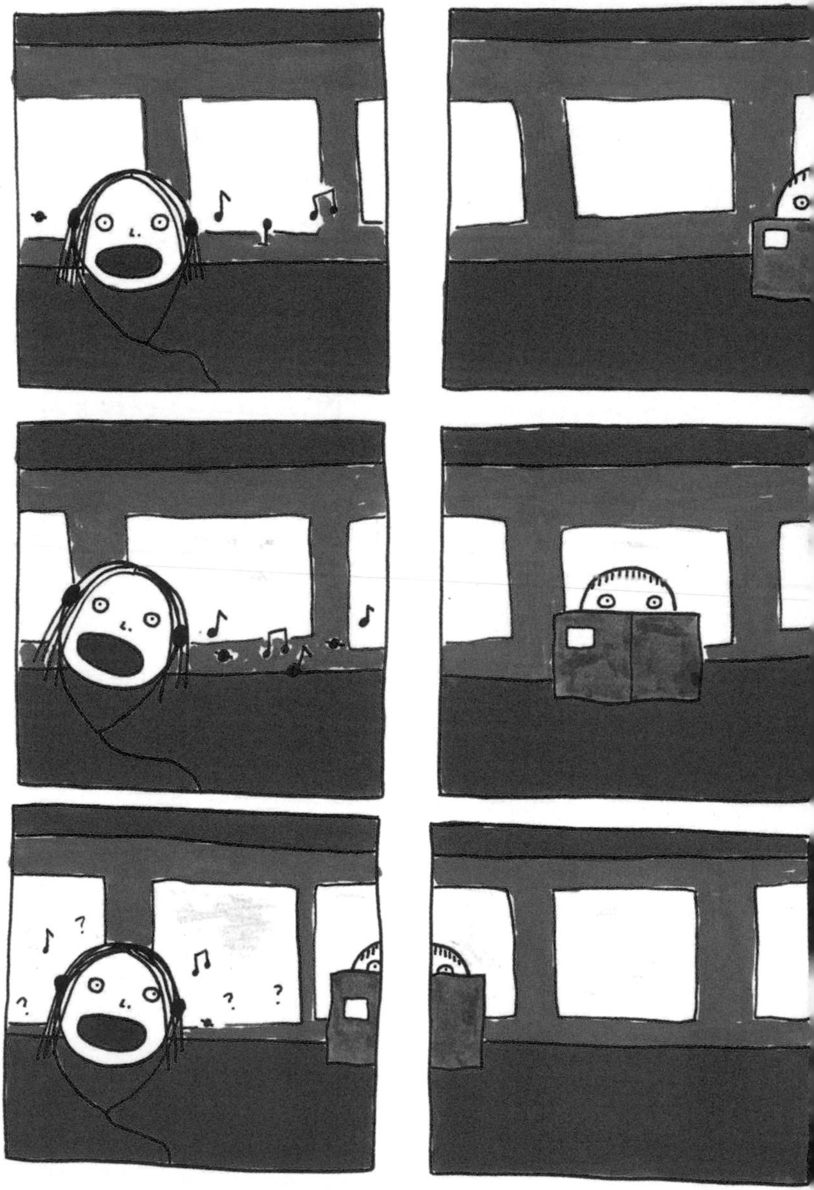

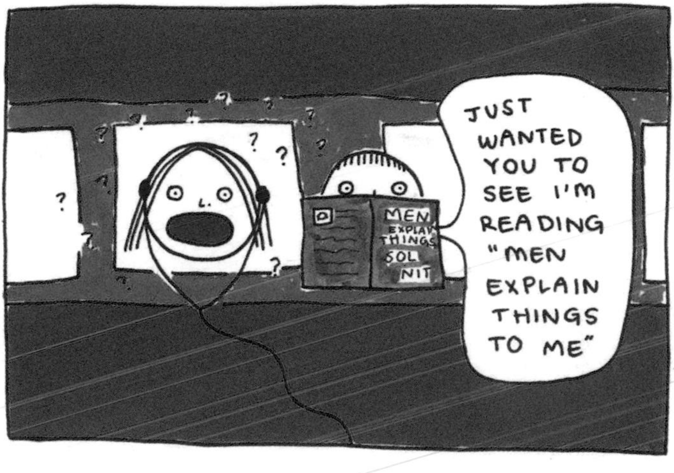
MEN
EXPLAI
THINGS
SOL
NIT
JUST WANTED YOU TO SEE I'M READING "MEN EXPLAIN THINGS TO ME"

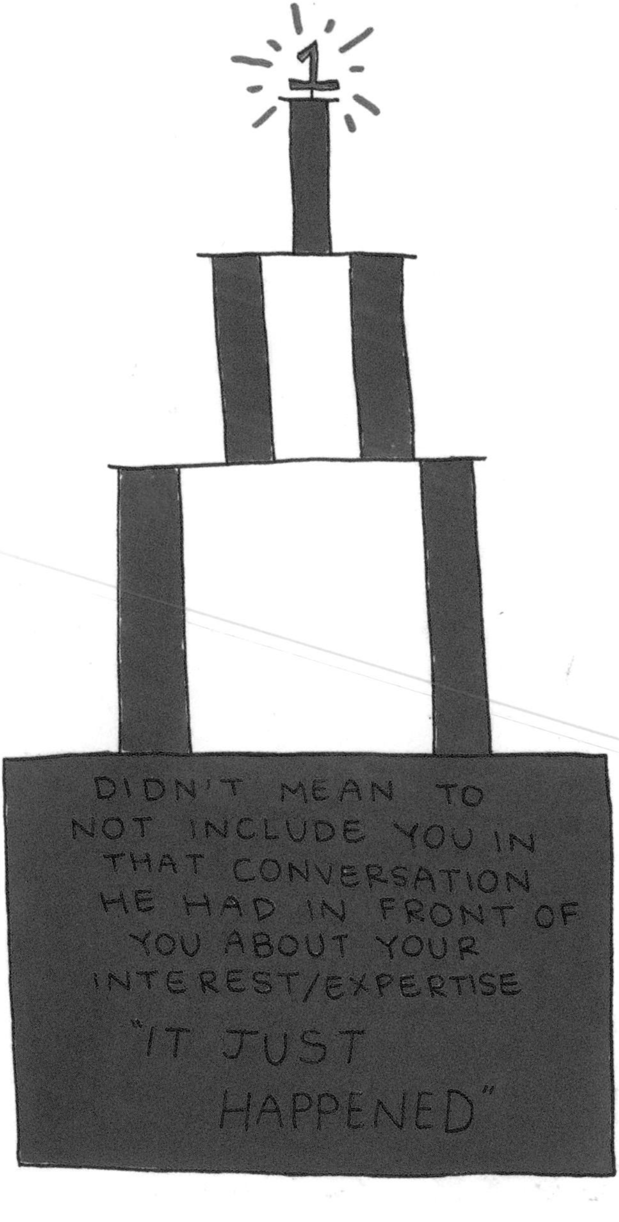
1
DIDN'T MEAN TO NOT INCLUDE YOU IN THAT CONVERSATION HE HAD IN FRONT OF YOU ABOUT YOUR INTEREST/EXPERTISE
"IT JUST HAPPENED"

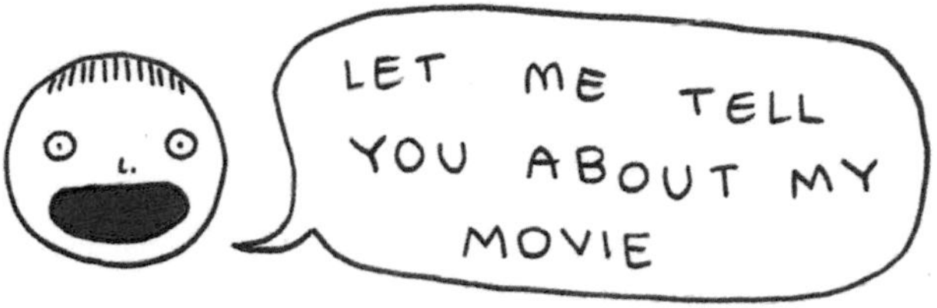
LET ME TELL YOU ABOUT MY MOVIE

DATE WHO FORCED ME TO WALK ACROSS THE WILLIAMSBURG BRIDGE

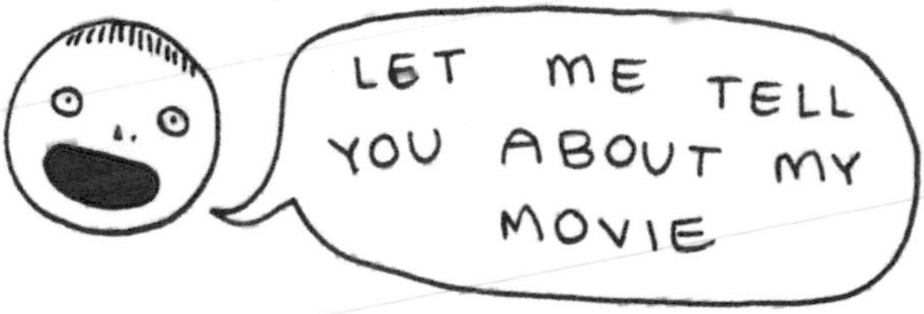
LET ME TELL YOU ABOUT MY MOVIE

DATE WITH WHOM MY ONLY MUTUAL FRIEND ON TINDER WAS MY EX, KISSED ME AND THEN NEVER TEXTED, SAW ME AT A BAR MONTHS AFTER AND MADE SEARING EYE CONTACT WITH ME, IGNORED ME

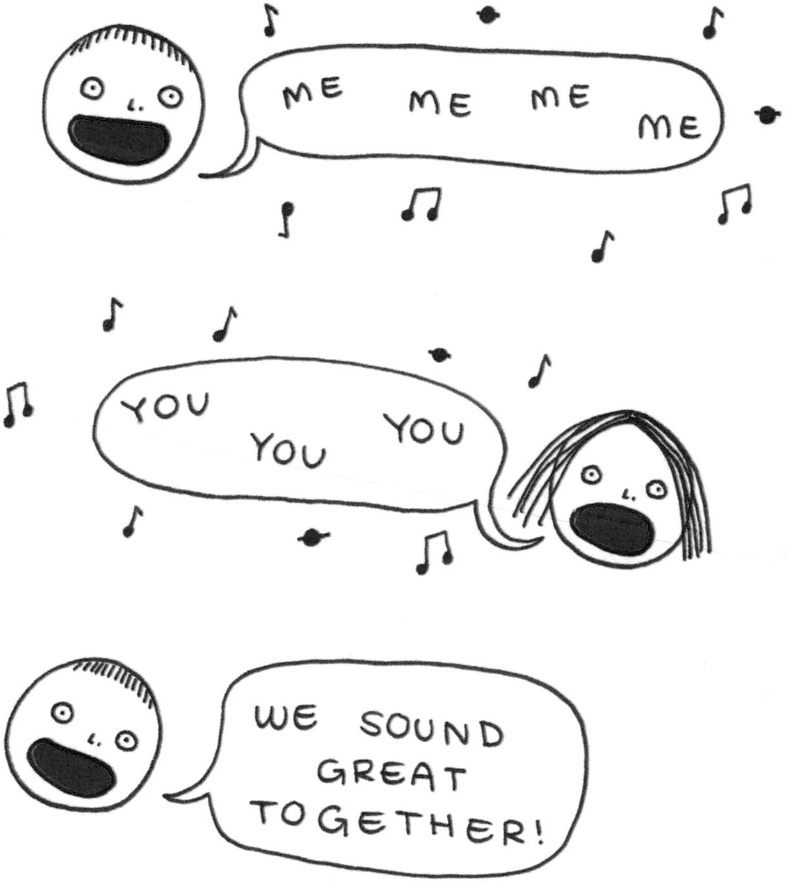
ME ME ME ME
YOU YOU YOU
WE SOUND GREAT TOGETHER!

CATCALL,
BUT MAKE IT FASHION

tat·calling
noun

THE PHENOMENON OF PEOPLE, USUALLY
CIS DUDES, USING SOMEONE'S TATTOOS
AS A WAY TO JUSTIFY / EXCUSE /
RATIONALIZE OTHERWISE INAPPROPRIATE
BEHAVIOR SUCH AS NONCONSENSUAL
TOUCHING OR UNSOLICITED "FEEDBACK"
ABOUT SOMEONE ELSE'S BODY

Good boys don't catcall. They would never. Good god!

But they *will* tat-call, among other creative methods through which they convey the vital message "I'M LOOKING AT YOUR BODY" without, you know, being *creepy* about it.

This is a common good-boy-logic loophole, like playing a game of Twister around what one knows they should do versus what they "just can't help" doing. It seems good boys believe that if they can find a way to let you know they're looking at your body without *directly* objectifying your body—because not what a good boy does, and also, they know they won't be successful with the ladies these days with that take—they're in the clear! So they opt for an adjacent flattening of your being into a consumable entity, obviously existing only to satisfy *their* gaze/desire/sexual yearnings, irrespective of your own. They've done it! They've released their important opinion into the universe and asserted authority over your body but, crucially, they can still rest easy at night like the sweet little boys they are. Not a creep. Nailed it.

After posting about this phenomenon on Instagram, I was mildly surprised it was seen as controversial. One tattoo artist chimed in: "you shouldn't get tattoos if you don't want people to comment on them." Sir? I did not get my tattoos to broadcast to the world: EVERYBODY, COME ON DOWN AND LET'S CHAT! I got them for myself, specifically in moments where doing something of permanence with my body was a powerful form of self-love and ownership. For me, when people scream "Good tats!" from across the street or inexplicably take my tattoos as permission to touch me, the message reads loud and clear, to me, as YOUR BODY IS MINE FOR CONSUMPTION, and then, if challenged, I WAS ONLY LOOKING AT THE AESTHETICS ALL OVER YOUR BODY CALM DOWN.

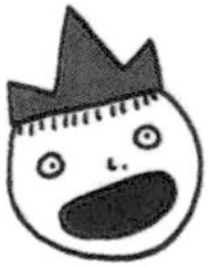

HEY, IT'S THE GASLIGHT KING AGAIN!

Some people like to talk about their tattoos with strangers and wouldn't be offended by, perhaps would even love, being told in passing, "Great tats." That's cool. Nothing wrong with that. People have different needs. Different things feel good for different people. Which makes it fairly obvious, to me, that using SHOUT! THAT! UNSOLICITED! OPINION! as a one-size-fits-most model is woefully ignorant of the complexities of our differing needs.

STOOD UP FOR A FEMALE COLLEAGUE
ALONE IN THE BATHROOM
TO THE MIRROR

PLEASE, BOYS, BE MORE CONSCIOUS OF THE SPACE YOU TAKE UP
SPACE ...

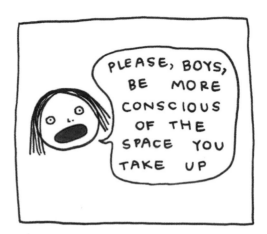

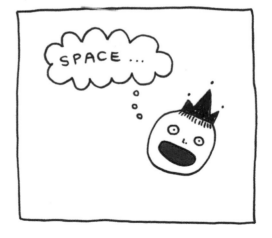

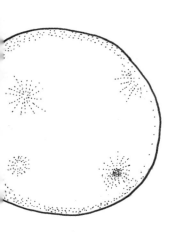

BREAKING: BRIAN
MOVING BRILANDIA
TO SPACE

↑ A MOON

HERE I GO!

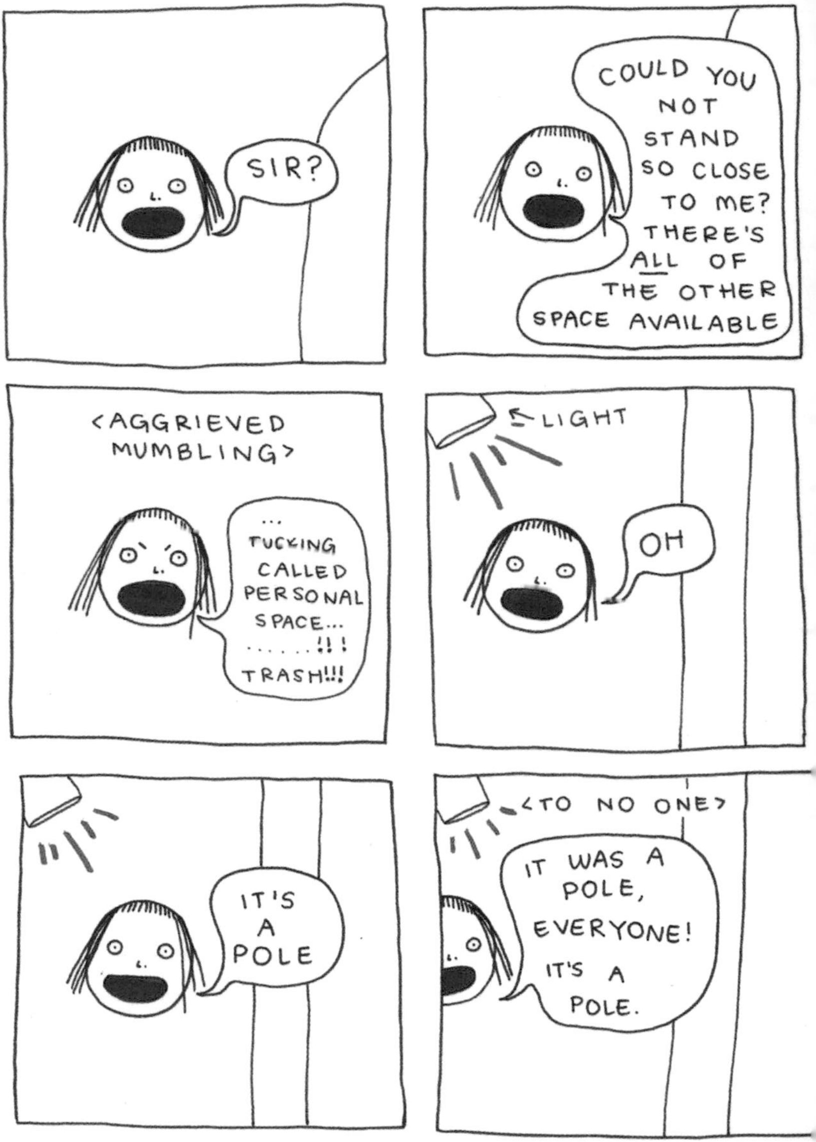
SIR?
COULD YOU NOT STAND SO CLOSE TO ME? THERE'S ALL OF THE OTHER SPACE AVAILABLE
<AGGRIEVED MUMBLING>
... TUCKING CALLED PERSONAL SPACE... ....!!! TRASH!!!
LIGHT
OH
IT'S A POLE
<TO NO ONE>
IT WAS A POLE, EVERYONE! IT'S A POLE.

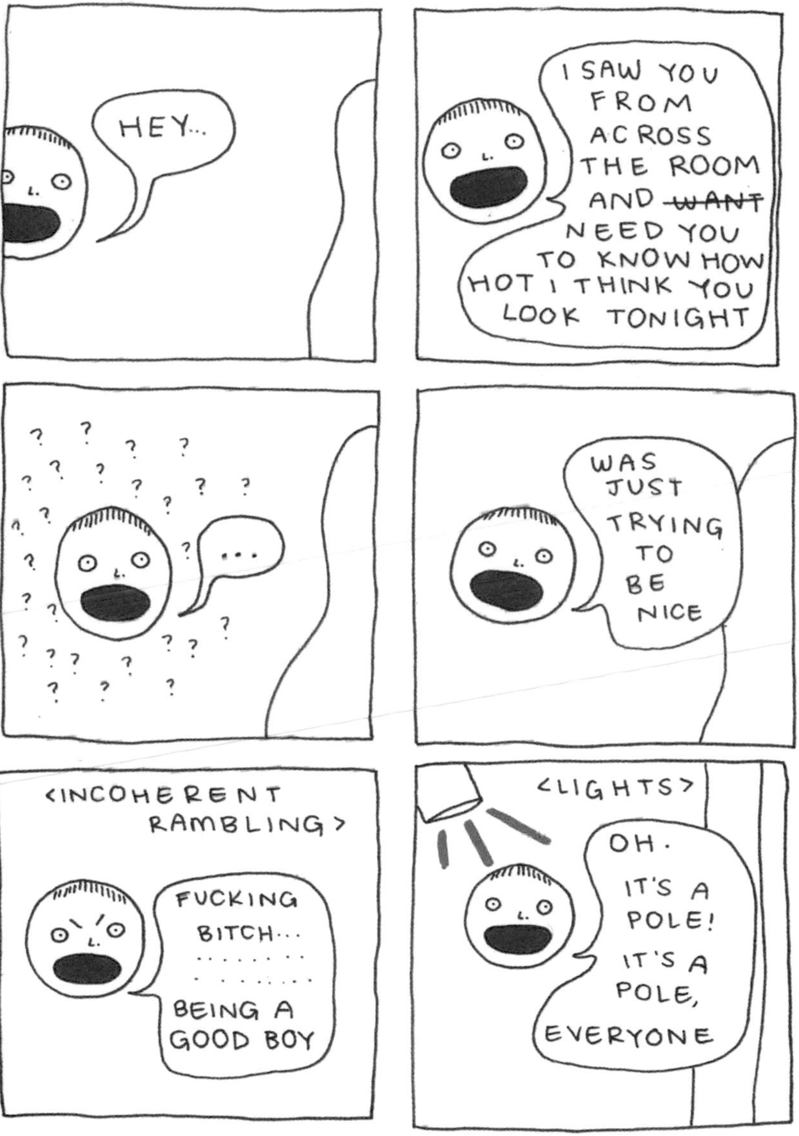
HEY...
I SAW YOU FROM ACROSS THE ROOM AND ~~WANT~~ NEED YOU TO KNOW HOW HOT I THINK YOU LOOK TONIGHT
...
WAS JUST TRYING TO BE NICE
<INCOHERENT RAMBLING>
FUCKING BITCH... .... BEING A GOOD BOY
<LIGHTS>
OH. IT'S A POLE! IT'S A POLE, EVERYONE

YE OLDE CATCALL CONFUSION

IT ALWAYS CONFUSES ME SO WHEN LADS COURT ME WHILST GALLOPING BY? IS IT TO IMPRESS ME WITH THINE SPEEDY STEED? BUT IF SO, THEY HAVE UNDERMINED THEIR OWN COURTSHIP, FOR EVEN IF I <u>WERE</u> TO FLASH A HINT OF ANKLE, HE HAS LONG RIDDEN OFF

<TO EVERYONE>

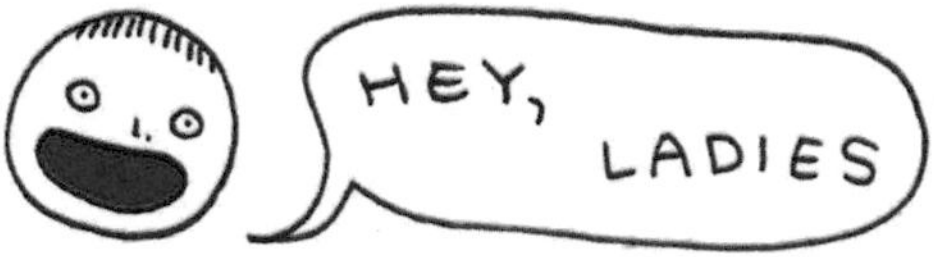
HEY, LADIES

<POINTED AT ME>

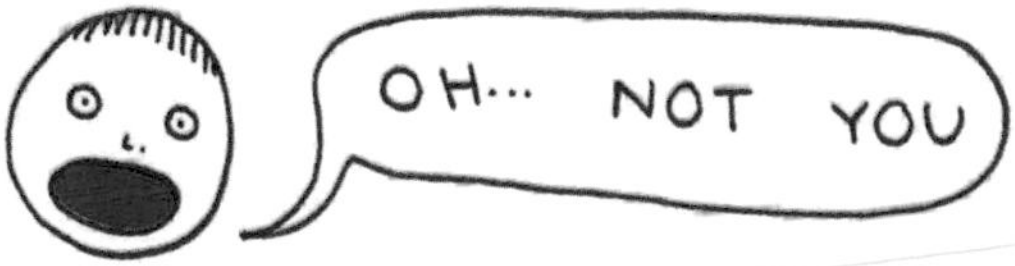
OH... NOT YOU

ONCE A GROUP OF MEN CATCALLED A BUNCH OF GIRLS I WAS WITH. THEY RESPECTFULLY SPARED ME THE HARASSMENT BY POINTING AT ME AND SHOUTING, "BUT NOT YOU!"

A VERY ABRIDGED LOOK AT WHAT MEN HAVE SAID ABOUT MY WORK ONLINE
UGLY, BUT FUNNY
YOU'RE LIKE THE MICHAEL JORDAN OF PASSIVE AGGRESSIVENESS
YOU LOOK LIKE ADRIAN BRODY
I DON'T THINK OF YOUR ART AS ART
YOU'RE JUST BITCHING AND COMPLAINING
DO YOU HATE ALL MEN THOUGH?
BE NICER
WOW IMAGINE IF A DUDE MADE THIS. DOUBLE STANDARD

BITTER ASSHOLE
NOT AS FUNNY AS DUDES LOL
PETTY BITCH
YOU'VE MADE A VACUOUS MANHATING ECHO CHAMBER
UNFUNNY CUNT, LOL
DATES LOSERS, VILIFIES THEM, SELLS MERCH. YOU MUST BE A REAL PRIZE
AHHHHH HHHH HHHHH HHHH HHH
OVERREACTING
YOUR SEX LIFE MUST BE SO SAD

ASKS HOW YOU'RE DOING!
ONCE EVERY THIRD FULL MOON
WHEN THE WIND BLOWS DUE NORTH
AND THE PLANETS ARE
ALIGNED JUST SO
(WITHIN 30° OF EACH OTHER,
WHICH, IF YOU INCLUDE PLUTO—
WHICH I DO — OCCURS ROUGHLY
EVERY 500 YEARS)

CHAPTER 4

PYGMALION

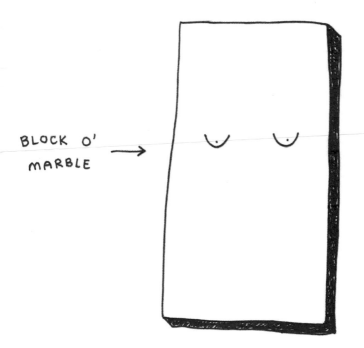

BLOCK O'
MARBLE →

PYGMALION

OH FUCK I THINK MY CURRENT
BOYFRIEND IS PYGMALIONING
THE SHIT OUT OF ME?

— MUSINGS FOUND IN AN
OLD NOTEBOOK

In college, I was in a long-distance "open" (more on that later) relationship with a boy a few years older than me who lived in New York, while I was finishing up school in Ohio. I received an unyielding stream of content about his own life that he released into the void of our primarily digital exchanges, demanding validation—being seen, being asked follow-up questions. Though he gave little in return, I told myself if I poured enough love and emotional labor into him, he would turn around and show me the same.

In many ways, I was dating him because I wanted his life. His cool job. His ability to make money as an artist, doing what he loved. I knew, but decided not to notice, that he conveniently ignored the fact that I was an artist, too, because I was young and not "a professional" like him and my art and words came from a place of my own vulnerability and—gasp—emotionality. He was very much a LOGIC OR BUST sort of man. And I was drawn to that, too, because #internalizedmisogyny told me my version of seeing the world was less than, and his was the North Star I should seek to follow.

The short version is: he didn't want me as a partner. He wanted me as a cheerleader. Someone to *inspire* him, to make him feel needed and loved and worthy, to keep him company while he waited for someone more suitable—not in college, not so *emotional*—to come along.

During this time, I found comfort in ye olde versions of my current boyfriend: other old, white men and their art, who shined a light on the fucked-up-ness of my then-percolating ideas about men and their desires.

I got most stuck on Ovid's "Pygmalion." It's a story you recognize, though likely not by that name. (*My Fair Lady* is a more modern example, as is the film *Let's Get Away With a Lot Of Suspect Sex-Robot Politics by Filming This Edgily*, also called *Ex Machina*).

Pygmalion is from a collection of myths called *Metamorphoses*, each about transformation of a sinister, specific kind: men/gods changing living women into voiceless, bodiless, inhuman beings. In one myth, Apollo turns Daphne into a laurel tree, and as soon as she's finally not such a pesky human being with agency, he breaks a limb off her tree-body AND MAKES IT INTO A FUCKING CROWN for himself. I was obsessed with how literal it all was: So many levels of male author and male hero using women for their stories, crowning themselves with women and their bodies. Story after story of men (ab)using their muses to validate and uphold their own worth.

But Pygmalion is the exception. His story works a bit differently.

The myth begins with our main man Pygmalion, a sculptor, wandering through town expressing his disgust with women. It's like an angsty coming-of-age movie for toxic masculinity: head leaning against a cart (I don't know, bear with me) as a pastoral rush of images whips past, some indie soundtrack setting the mood for his pivotal realization: "Real women are shit." (I'm paraphrasing here.)

Have no fear! He's an artist! Old white dude artists are notoriously chill! Which is why he promptly goes back to his studio and sculpts himself a better woman. A stoic woman with no demands because, wow! She's made of marble! He prays to Venus for his statue, Galatea, to come to life, which she grants. This seems momentarily cool because FUCK YEAH VENUS YOU'VE GOT THE POWER but alas, nope, Ovid's still writing this. Pygmalion and his now-alive statue then fuck and have a child.

Pygmalion, and the persistence of this myth, reflects something too true about the world, about men and their desires, real or imagined, taught or inherited or enforced. He doesn't sculpt a better father or mother or gender-neutral lover or friend. He doesn't sculpt a dog, which would have been awesome. He sculpts a woman—a hot one—born of perceived necessity due to the failures of real women. He crafts for himself a muse, model, sex object, magnum opus with a mouth. He sculpts the figment of woman: unfeeling, distant, pure potential. The perfect woman is not about her shape, not about her contents, but, in this realm and in so many others, about her readiness to be molded into the version that best suits the man shaping her.

* * *

I knew I was being flattened in the relationship I was in when I read these myths. I knew he was taking from me, in the way he talked at me, made my own achievements smaller, forced me to drive all the Big Conversations if I wanted any clarity about what we were doing, manipulated me into essentially breaking up with myself so he could pursue his new, more serious, girlfriend. I knew my own complexities were being erased in favor of a role oriented around his tool—the literal, as in his dick, and the figurative, as in his metaphorical chisel—and that to contradict this was to threaten the comfort of whatever the fuck it was I thought we had.

I stayed with him anyway. It is an odd feeling, knowing you are walking in someone else's imagining of you, which you fit closely. But it's not right. "Intellectual knowledge"—the clarity of what you should do—is cleaved from what your heart tells you to do. So there you are, inhabiting a self that's adjacent to you, that more closely parallels the needs of someone else. I sat back and watched as I became a me that wasn't me, a me that was compromised, a me that was smaller.

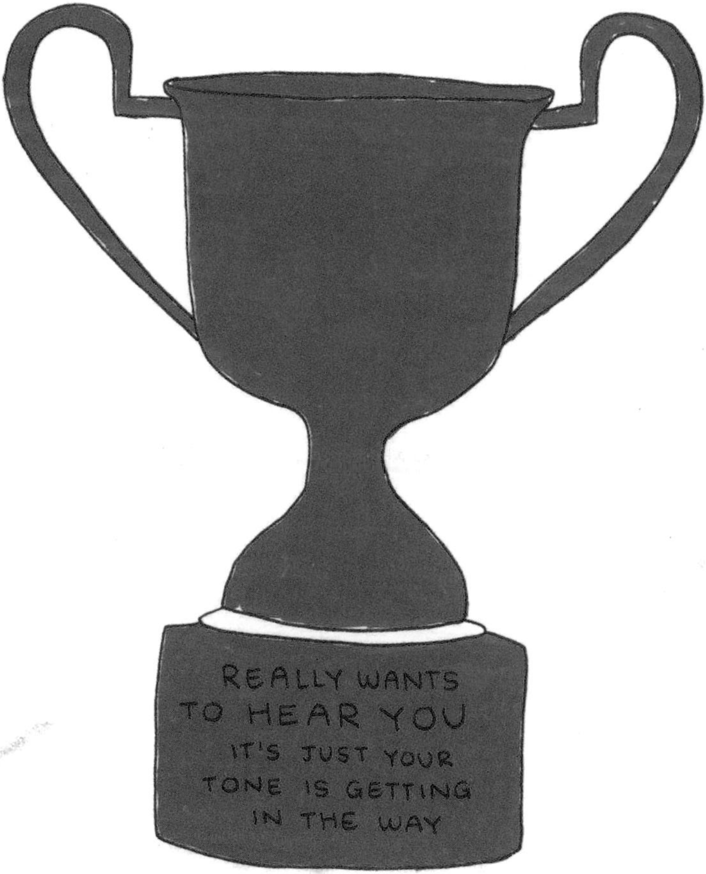
REALLY WANTS
TO HEAR YOU
IT'S JUST YOUR
TONE IS GETTING
IN THE WAY

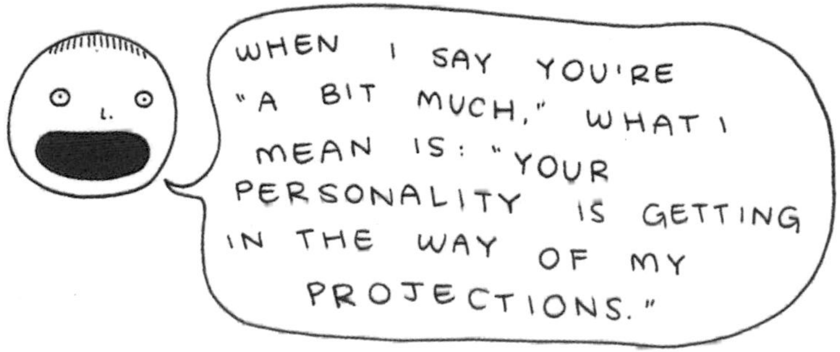
WHEN I SAY YOU'RE "A BIT MUCH," WHAT I MEAN IS: "YOUR PERSONALITY IS GETTING IN THE WAY OF MY PROJECTIONS."

SUPPORTS OTHER
FEMINISTS*

* AS LONG AS THEY'RE THE
"CUTE" KIND AND NOT LIKE,
TRYING TO DISRUPT
THE STATUS QUO WITH
THEIR WHOLE "MEAN
BITTER MAN-HATING BITCHES"
SCHTICK

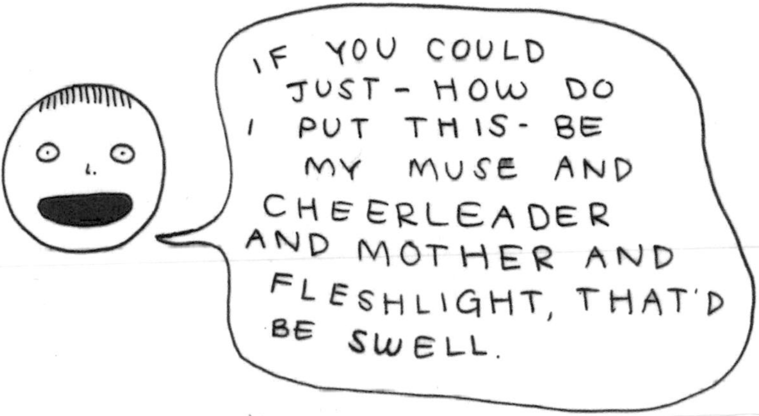
IF YOU COULD JUST - HOW DO I PUT THIS - BE MY MUSE AND CHEERLEADER AND MOTHER AND FLESHLIGHT, THAT'D BE SWELL.

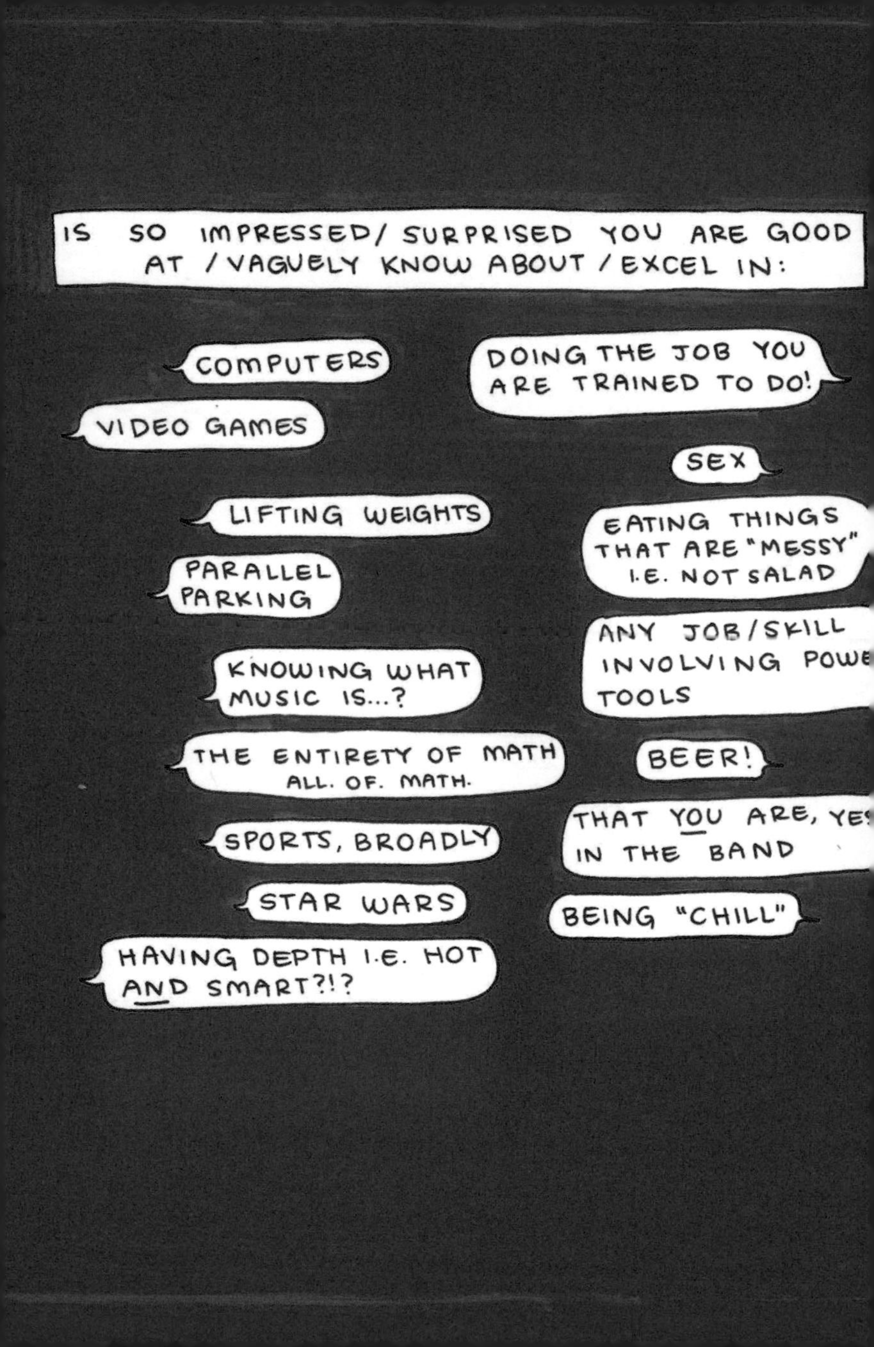
IS SO IMPRESSED/ SURPRISED YOU ARE GOOD AT / VAGUELY KNOW ABOUT / EXCEL IN:
COMPUTERS
VIDEO GAMES
LIFTING WEIGHTS
PARALLEL PARKING
KNOWING WHAT MUSIC IS...?
THE ENTIRETY OF MATH ALL. OF. MATH.
SPORTS, BROADLY
STAR WARS
HAVING DEPTH I.E. HOT AND SMART?!?
DOING THE JOB YOU ARE TRAINED TO DO!
SEX
EATING THINGS THAT ARE "MESSY" I.E. NOT SALAD
ANY JOB/SKILL INVOLVING POWE TOOLS
BEER!
THAT YOU ARE, YE IN THE BAND
BEING "CHILL"

I LUMP "VAGUELY KNOW ABOUT" AND "EXCEL" TOGETHER BECAUSE TO MANY A GOOD BOY IT DOESN'T SEEM TO MATTER, SO CAPTIVATED ARE THEY BY THE NOVELTY OF A SEX OBJECT UNCANNILY REVEALING THEMSELVES TO BE THREE-DIMENSIONAL.

I HAD HEARD "YOU'RE ACTUALLY REALLY FUNNY" LONG BEFORE I WAS PROFESSIONALLY FUNNY AND I HEAR IT STILL.

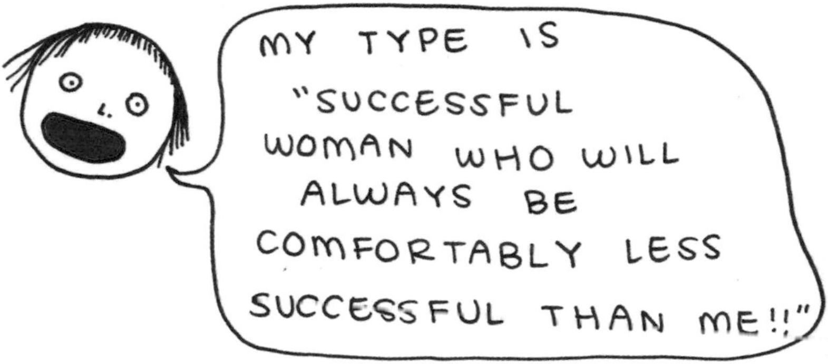
MY TYPE IS "SUCCESSFUL WOMAN WHO WILL ALWAYS BE COMFORTABLY LESS SUCCESSFUL THAN ME!!"

NOT LIKE OTHER GIRLS"

Another giveaway of a Pygmalion is a boy's surprise when you display traits that betray the image he has projected onto you.

"Did you just come up with this?" men have asked me about my quick, witty responses. I'm a professional writer. It is quite literally my job to *come up* with things.

What are they doing besides trying to turn their own subverted, condescending expectations into a compliment? They're like, *You've inched above what I imagined you could be, which wasn't much. Hot.*

Often, this makes you "not like other girls." When guys say this, they seem to think it's a compliment, but it rests on an insult in all directions. Girls that do societally coded "feminine" things are "basic," whereas you, you edgy little dream, resist and dare to like *Lord of the Rings* or "cool music" or math (I mean, come on) and therefore become a sexy mess of contradictions.

This occurs frequently in tandem with reductive thinking around race, class, gender identity, sexuality. "You're hot for a [insert: fat girl, black girl, trans girl]," a man will say, offering unsolicited "praise" for being fuckable despite his own prejudices.

Of course, this all rests on our ability to still, ultimately, conform to the heart of their preconceived notions. To gently nudge the edges of expectations is hot and sexy and chic; to be too good at defying them is to pose a threat. To be too successful, too strong, too dominant, too angry, too unwomanly, too unmanly, too nothing, too everything is to disrupt the illusion of the man as the one who sets the rules, who holds the chisel.

THINKS
YOU'D LOOK
REALLY PRETTY
IF YOU LOST
A FEW POUNDS^x

ˣNOT TO͟O MUCH WEIGHT LOSS. JUST
LIKE... IN THE RIGHT PLACES. LIKE STAY
TITTED, GET TONED.

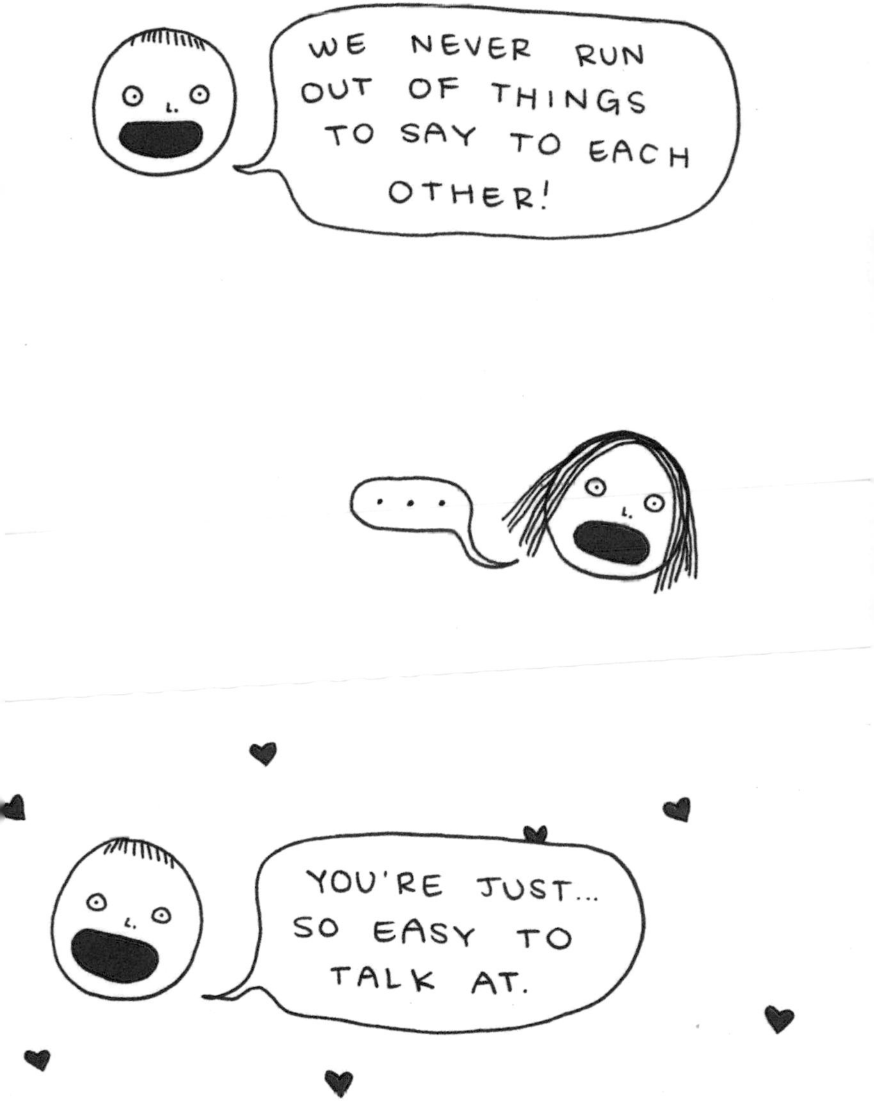
WE NEVER RUN OUT OF THINGS TO SAY TO EACH OTHER!
. . .
YOU'RE JUST... SO EASY TO TALK AT.

DIGITAL PYGMALION

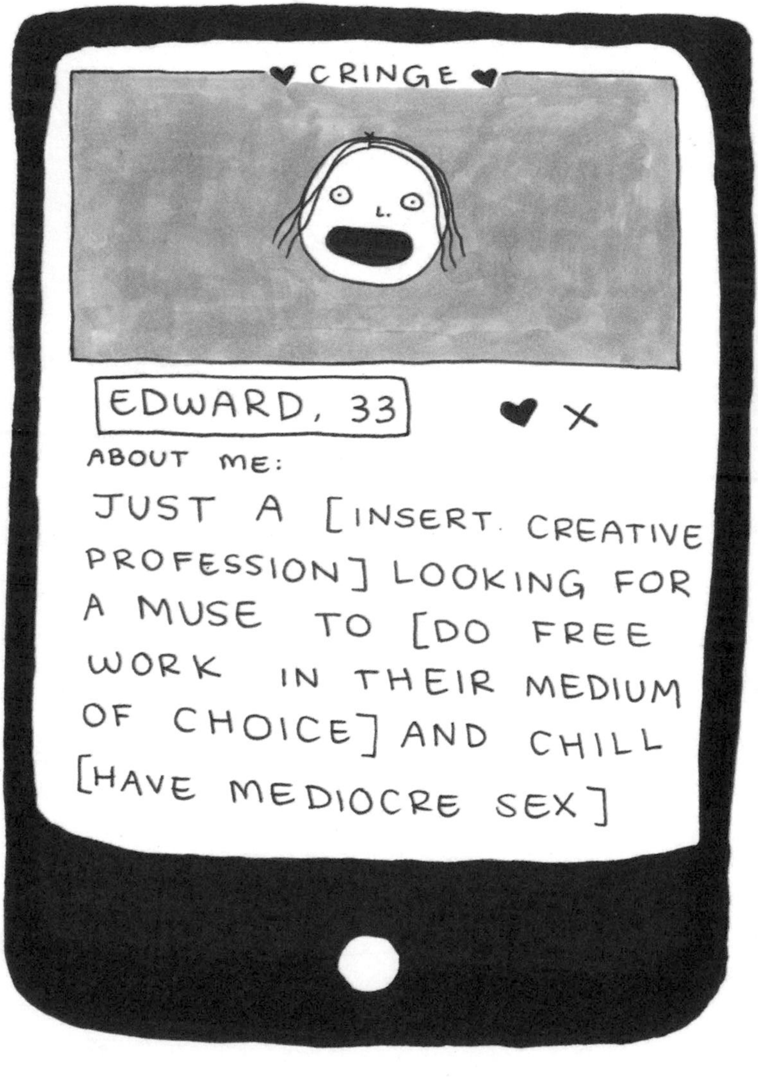

CRINGE
EDWARD, 33
ABOUT ME:
JUST A [INSERT CREATIVE PROFESSION] LOOKING FOR A MUSE TO [DO FREE WORK IN THEIR MEDIUM OF CHOICE] AND CHILL [HAVE MEDIOCRE SEX]

WOMEN ALSO SHAPE OTHER WOMEN TO BE MORE PLEASING SHAPES FOR MEN:

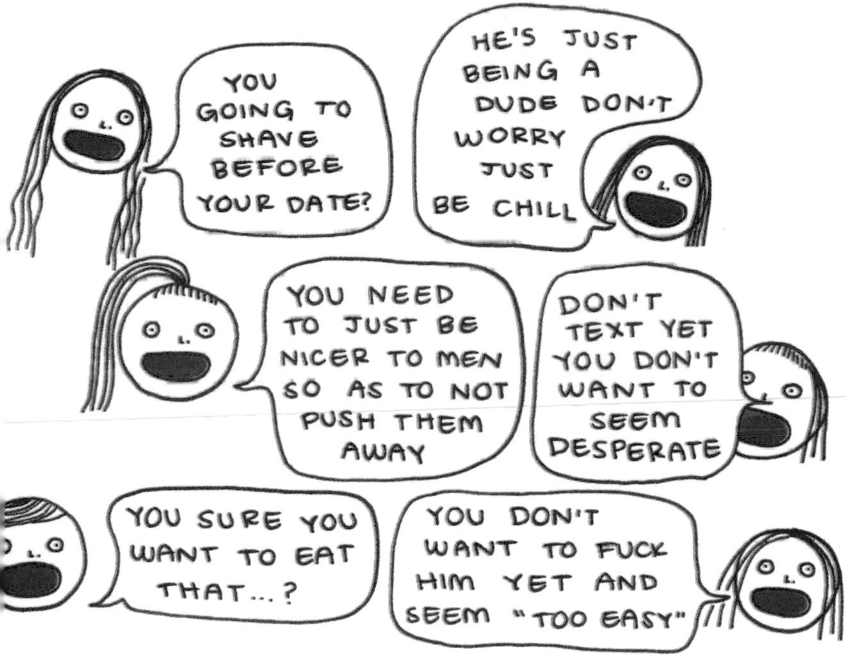
YOU GOING TO SHAVE BEFORE YOUR DATE?
HE'S JUST BEING A DUDE DON'T WORRY JUST BE CHILL
YOU NEED TO JUST BE NICER TO MEN SO AS TO NOT PUSH THEM AWAY
DON'T TEXT YET YOU DON'T WANT TO SEEM DESPERATE
YOU SURE YOU WANT TO EAT THAT...?
YOU DON'T WANT TO FUCK HIM YET AND SEEM "TOO EASY"

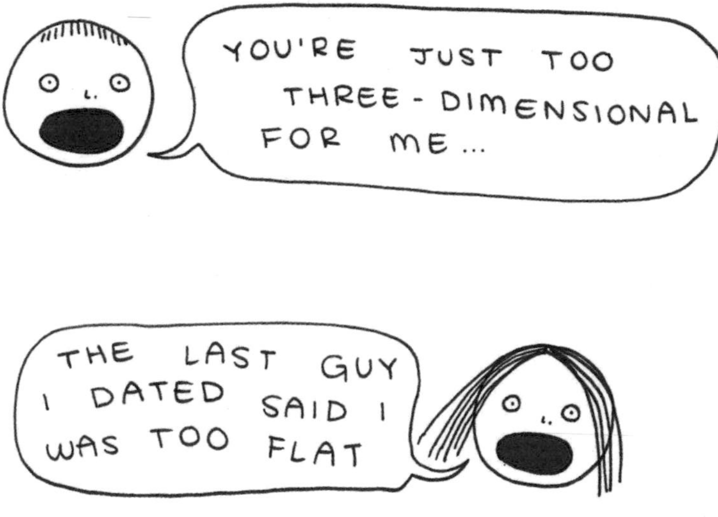
YOU'RE JUST TOO THREE-DIMENSIONAL FOR ME...
THE LAST GUY I DATED SAID I WAS TOO FLAT

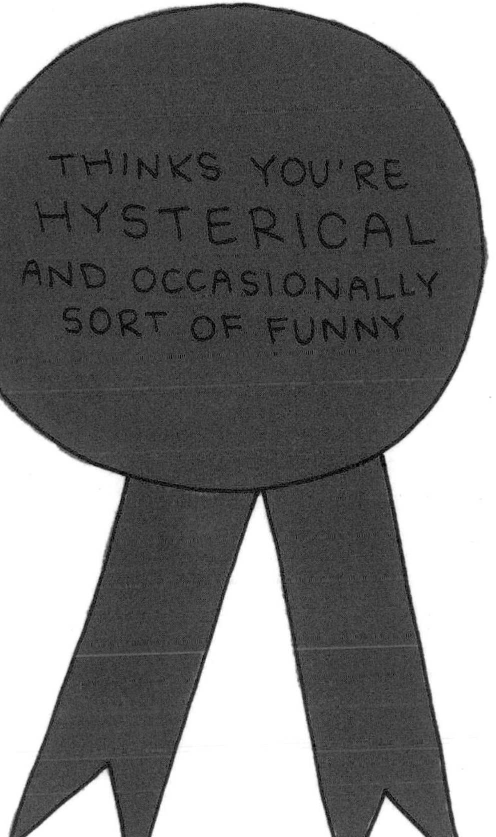
THINKS YOU'RE
HYSTERICAL
AND OCCASIONALLY
SORT OF FUNNY

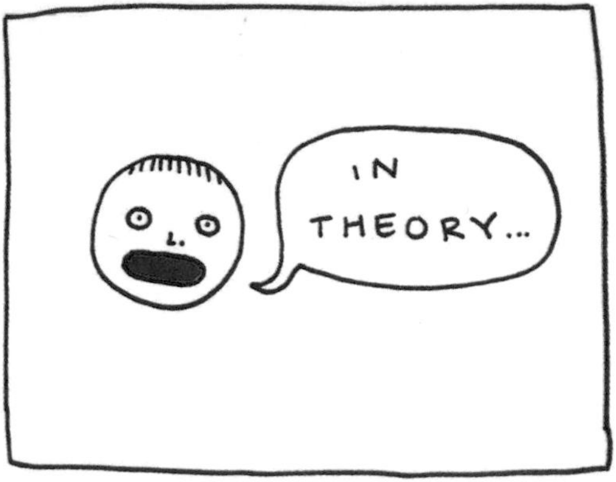
IN THEORY...

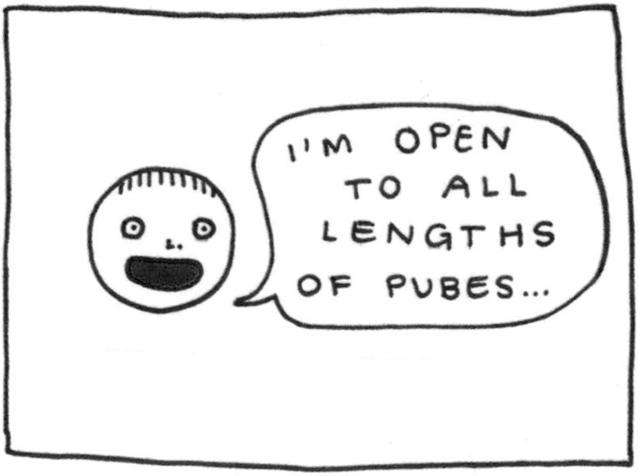
I'M OPEN TO ALL LENGTHS OF PUBES...

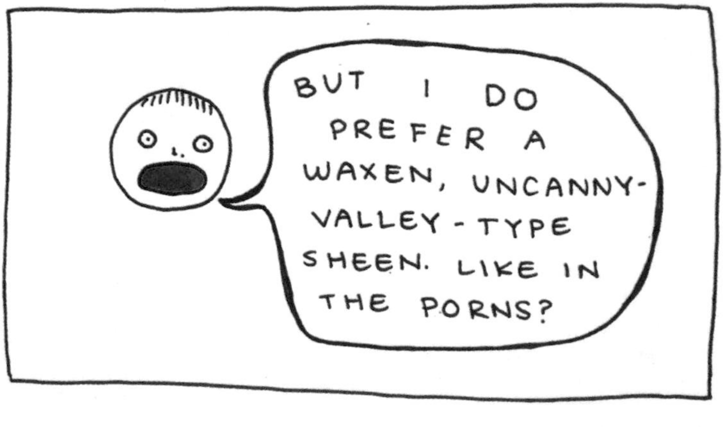
BUT I DO PREFER A WAXEN, UNCANNY-VALLEY-TYPE SHEEN. LIKE IN THE PORNS?

CHAPTER 5

REVERSE PYGMALION

‹MUFFLED›
I'M EMOTIONALLY AVAILABLE SOMEWHERE IN HERE! LIKE A GEODE! GET TO WORK!

REVERSE PYGMALION

(OR, ALL THE PARTNERS I'VE SCULPTED INTO BETTER PARTNERS FOR SOMEONE WHO IS NOT ME)

"I'm just tired of these men I put on a pedestal for being so fucking amazing, because they are funny, or nice, or smart. I'm all those things yet they make me feel like waiting a million hours before getting a text back is a given because, unlike me, apparently, *they are busy and their time is worth guarding.* And when they *do* text back with some monosyllabic 'hey,' I get all happy? For what? Even their basic communication skills are things *I've taught and demanded from them.*"

This is a reenactment. But I suspect I was saying something like this to a friend, on a phone call in my parents' backyard, before a boy told me he was going to turn these words into a song. His song.

This is a meta story. It is also true—I promise.

I was talking to my friend specifically about how *I* was a Pygmalion, too, shaping and molding and crafting these men I dated, loved, because I saw in them something so dangerous: *potential.*

And then this boy in the adjacent yard popped his head over the fence and told me: "Hey, uh, I overheard your conversation, and I just wanted to let you know that I'm not like those guys, the ones you were talking about."

I was not quite prepared for what was happening or how it was being presented to me as a nice treat. Here was this stranger who had eavesdropped on a very intimate conversation and was not only confirming he had listened but using my hard-won revelations about myself to put himself on a pedestal above the other nameless boys in my life.

I think I just nodded, as one does, in such moments.

"I also, uh . . . you're really smart. So I took some notes as you were talking? I'm going to use them as lyrics for a song."

Oh, good! Definitely use my words about how much emotional labor I put into men for your own shitty song. The irony is so thick. It's molasses irony.

This was not the first time, and would definitely not be the last, that men for whom I gracefully modeled normal human behavior would go on to co-opt that work for their own gain. Some of that work, like in actual partnerships, of course, is mutual. We change and shape and grow with each other, for each other.

But this . . . this was not that.

This is a VERY literal example of the emotional labor I've done for men, wittingly and unwittingly. For years I crafted men into better people and never got to reap the benefits. I saw their many red flags—like emotional unavailability—not as glaring signals to run but as opportunities to stay and fix them. To make them better.

I didn't have it all figured out then, and I don't know for sure that I do now. During the years in which I gave up so much of myself to men, I failed to account for the needs of my friends, my work, my self-growth in ways I am still reconciling. So normalized is the process of putting work into men, no one seemed phased by my questionable priorities. So conditioned was I to doing hours of emotional labor that I didn't think of what I wanted. Even when men weren't directly chiseling me and my shape and my contents, they didn't need to: I, like so many others, learned how to do it for them.

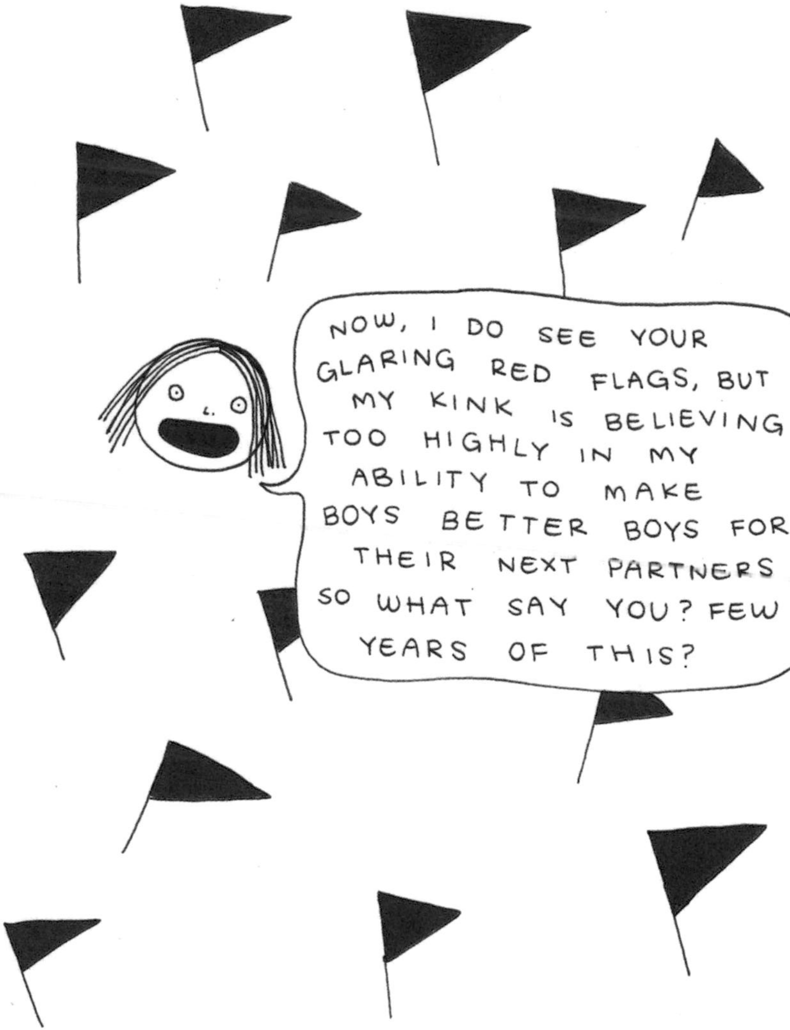
NOW, I DO SEE YOUR GLARING RED FLAGS, BUT MY KINK IS BELIEVING TOO HIGHLY IN MY ABILITY TO MAKE BOYS BETTER BOYS FOR THEIR NEXT PARTNERS SO WHAT SAY YOU? FEW YEARS OF THIS?

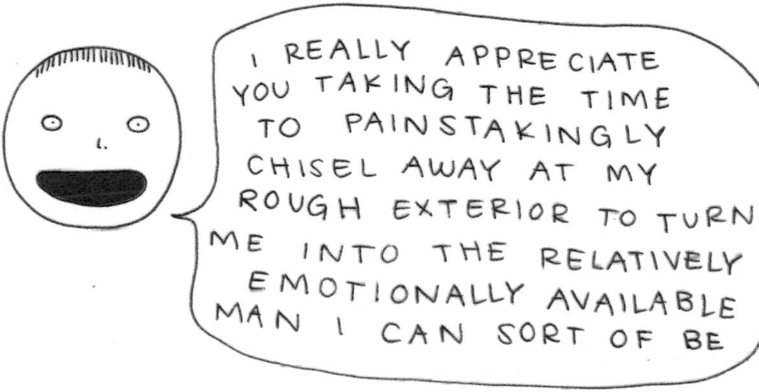
I REALLY APPRECIATE YOU TAKING THE TIME TO PAINSTAKINGLY CHISEL AWAY AT MY ROUGH EXTERIOR TO TURN ME INTO THE RELATIVELY EMOTIONALLY AVAILABLE MAN I CAN SORT OF BE

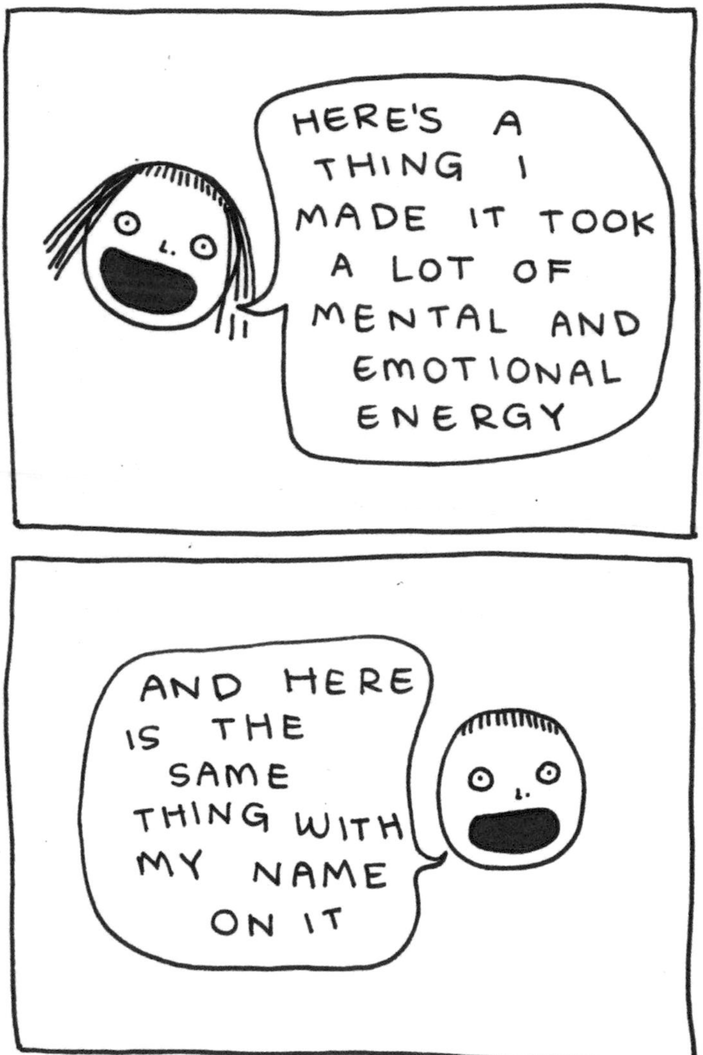
HERE'S A THING I MADE IT TOOK A LOT OF MENTAL AND EMOTIONAL ENERGY
AND HERE IS THE SAME THING WITH MY NAME ON IT

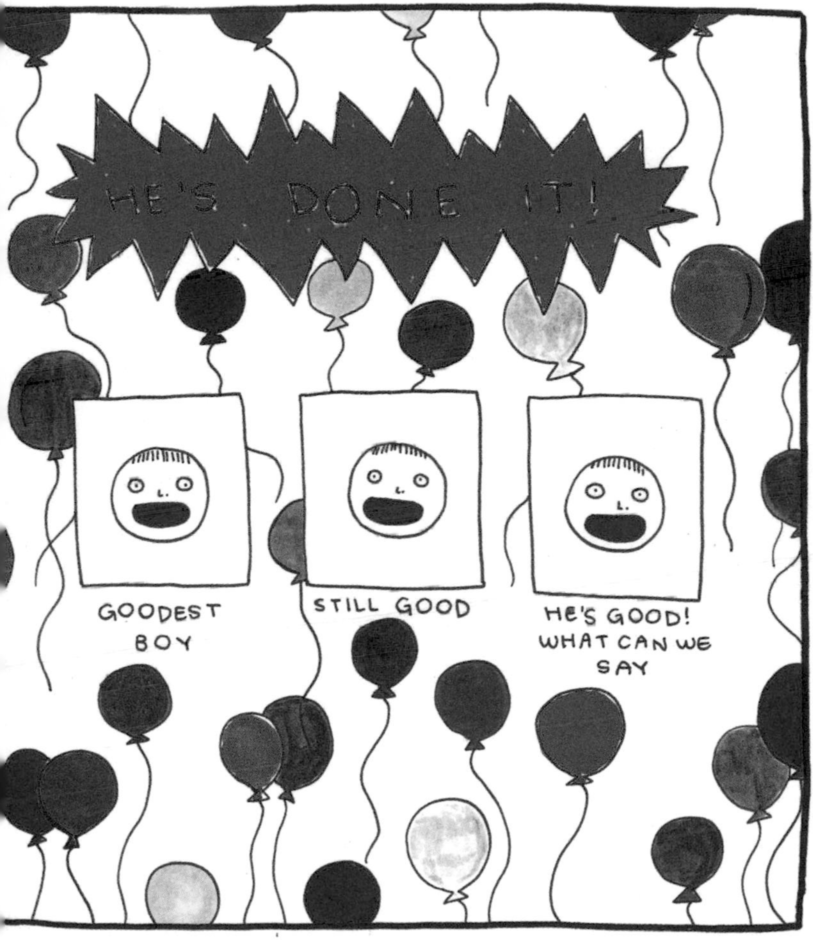
HE'S DONE IT!
GOODEST BOY
STILL GOOD
HE'S GOOD! WHAT CAN WE SAY

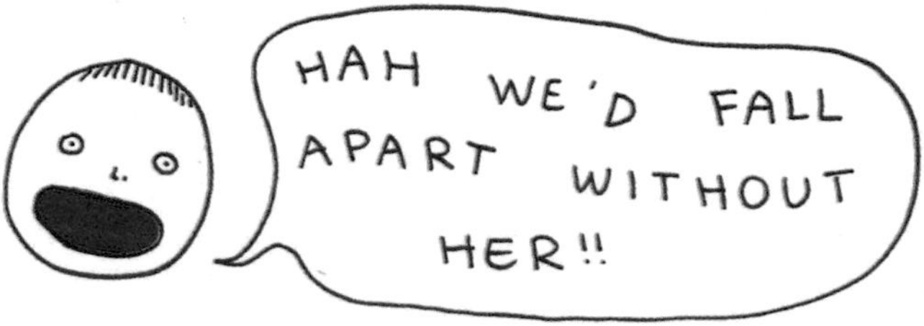
HAH WE'D FALL APART WITHOUT HER!!

HE SAID ABOUT AGATHA, THINKING HE WAS GIVING HER A COMPLIMENT, BUT, IN FACT, WAS REVEALING THE UNTOLD DEPTHS OF WORK AGATHA DID FOR HIM AND EVERYONE ELSE IN THE OFFICE FOR LESS MONEY

YE OLDE EMOTIONAL LABOR

IT WOULD SEEMST DESMOND HAS COME INTO TOWN MERELY TO BEMOAN HIS WORRIES AND ASK OF ME TO SOOTHE THEM, ASK NOTHING OF ME OR MINE TROUBLES, AND RIDE OFF A BETTERED MAN?

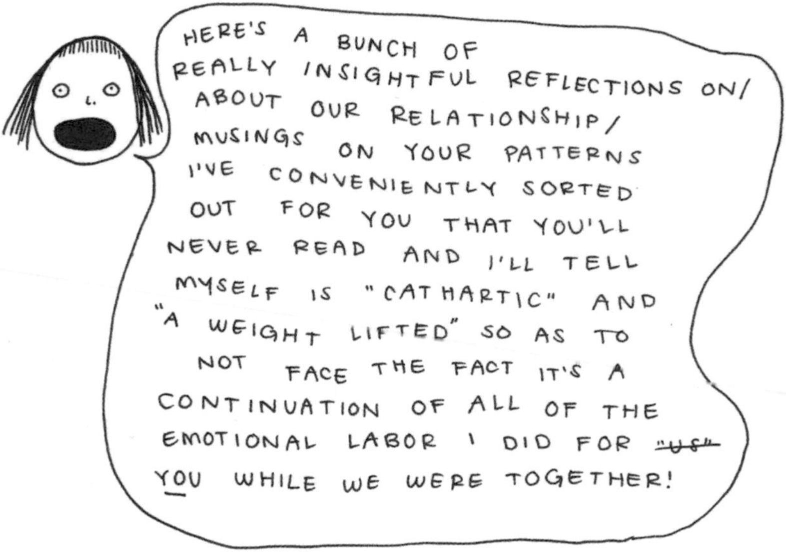
HERE'S A BUNCH OF REALLY INSIGHTFUL REFLECTIONS ON/ ABOUT OUR RELATIONSHIP/ MUSINGS ON YOUR PATTERNS I'VE CONVENIENTLY SORTED OUT FOR YOU THAT YOU'LL NEVER READ AND I'LL TELL MYSELF IS "CATHARTIC" AND "A WEIGHT LIFTED" SO AS TO NOT FACE THE FACT IT'S A CONTINUATION OF ALL OF THE EMOTIONAL LABOR I DID FOR ~~"US"~~ YOU WHILE WE WERE TOGETHER!

YOU OR THE TRASH

I ran into my ex—the one who was Pygmalioning the shit out of me—only twice, a near miracle given both of us were living in New York with adjacent social circles and a swath of shared spots and haunts.

The first time was the day I finally unfollowed him on Instagram. I had followed him *long* past what was healthy, mostly because I became a gleeful voyeur into his new relationship, interpreting his life as a performance of I'M IN A NEW RELATION-SHIP WITH NOT-SHELBY AND I'M SO MUCH HAPPIER. THANK YOU, SHELBY, FOR MAKING ME INTO SUCH A BETTER BOY SO I CAN BE A GREAT BOY FOR NOT-YOU. LOOK AT HOW MANY MUSEUMS WE GO TO. WE ARE SO HAPPY.

I should have cut off our social-media link when we ended things, but I desperately wanted to maintain a tenuous connection to him and tortured myself by exposing myself to it multiple times a day. It was not good for me; it prevented me from moving on and instilled in me a seedy resentment. I held on, anyway, until the day he made it easy by posting a video edit, complete with music and circa early-2000s video transitions such as slide and fade, of him MEETING. HIS. NEW. GIRLFRIEND'S. FAMILY. OVER. A SEAFOOD. BUFFET. The video was, like, 87 percent clams. That did it. I unfollowed while cackling grimly in McCarren Park in Brooklyn, awash in a mixture of *How could I have ever dated him?* and *Oh, fuck, I feel so alone.*

And then I saw him, mere minutes later, on the subway platform.

I wanted to say HELLO! THANK YOU SO MUCH FOR POSTING THAT CLAM VIDEO, IT WAS SO FREEING! ALSO? I KNOW YOU THINK YOU'RE A GOOD GUY AND WE "MUTUALLY" BROKE UP, BUT THAT'S A FUN LIE YOU TELL YOURSELF BECAUSE YOU ARE ACTUALLY A LYING SACK OF SHIT!

I didn't say anything, though. I watched him walk by. And when I got home, I did the only thing I know to do in these moments of utterly comic crisis: I started to write.

I wrote him an email but kept it in the drafts folder. It was a pretty typical Here's How You've Wronged Me and Are Still Wronging Me explainer, the type I send to nearly everyone I kiss (surprise!), finally addressing the facts I'd been hiding from for a year: that he was in a relationship with the woman he'd more or less left me for and only pretended we were still friends through calculatingly doled-out Instagram likes and occasional texts. I wrote that I knew these things now, and that the narrative he created to make himself feel okay about fucking me over was one he had forced me to inhabit with him, and that I was over it. Done.

The email sat in my drafts for months. I had never intended to send it—I told myself that he didn't deserve it, wouldn't respond. I questioned if releasing it into the universe would really help anything, anyway. It wouldn't, I decided.

And then one night I had a few glasses of red wine.

And then I sent the email.

* * *

Right after sending the email, I left to visit some friends at their apartment nearby. I was drunk on wine and on the release of finally sending the letter—it felt damn good to unleash something that had festered in my mind for so long. I got on the phone with my mom and sister and sauntered down my street.

I made it about two blocks before a man emerged onto his stoop and yelled "YOU!" at me.

Normally I would have kept walking but—again—drunk.

The man was holding a small black-and-white cat. They looked into my eyes—the man, knowingly, and the cat, bewilderedly. My mom and sister were still on the phone. I told them to hold on.

"You," he repeated. "You have to take this cat." He came down a few steps.

I was taken aback. This was, perhaps obviously, not what I was expecting from this exchange.

"No, sir, I'm really sorry, I can't take your cat," I said. "I live with a cat now." That seemed reasonable.

"I *know* you can take this cat." He said it with such an air of wisdom that I felt as if he knew something about *me* I didn't.

"No, I really . . . I can't take the cat. I'm headed to a friend's place, and I'm late, and I can't take the cat."

"You have to take this cat or I'm putting it in the garbage." He said this as he lowered the cat over a literal pile of trash.

GARBAGE

"There has to be a third option—"

"You or the trash."

By this point my mom and sister were losing their shit, laughing hysterically and offering solutions. "Call a shelter!" my sister said. "Can you take him to your apartment and keep him in the bathroom for a night?" my mom suggested.

I relayed the shelter idea. It did not go over well.

"He's a good cat. We just can't take care of him." The cat got lower. "You have to take this cat. *It's you or the trash.*"

"Okay, okay!" I shouted. "I'll take the cat!"

And then I took the cat.

I walked quickly away, announcing to my mom and sister, "I HAVE THE CAT. IT IS IN MY ARMS. I DON'T KNOW WHAT TO DO WITH THE CAT." We were all laughing, myself so hard I was crying, tears of joy and relief and confusion and utter disbelief.

Then it started pouring rain. I walked drunkenly for blocks, clutching a terrified cat and laughing, crying, snot pouring down my face. (I am also *very* allergic to cats.)

When I got to my friends' door, my face was a mask of absolute terror and confusion and apology—we were all supposed to be leaving their house shortly for shared plans—as I explained the saga of Trash Cat, as he was to be known for many months thereafter. I told them about how it had happened minutes after I'd sent the Here's How You Wronged Me email. That though he didn't deserve it, my words and brain and emotional labor, I ended up needing to release it, even knowing full well that he would never respond.

• • •

A week after I sent the email—eerily to the hour—I ran into my ex for the second and final time. He was across the street holding a too-big camera, his way of broadcasting his *did you know this is my super cool job?* job. I moved farther into his line of sight until he spotted me and approached.

"Hey, I got your email," he said. I was towering over him because in a rare moment of good fortune I had come from a party and was wearing heels. "It seemed like a murderer sent it. It was all lowercase."

That. That was the feedback he had for my extremely well-written "I'll be the adult about this" email reconciling our messy ending and calling him out for all the ways he had fucked up.

"I was going to respond, but I felt like the window closed," he said. Remember, this was ONE WEEK after I sent the email. THE WINDOW CLOSED.

"I'll call you soon, then," he finally said, the weirdness becoming overwhelming.

I asked, "Will you, though?"

He made a weird noise like this:

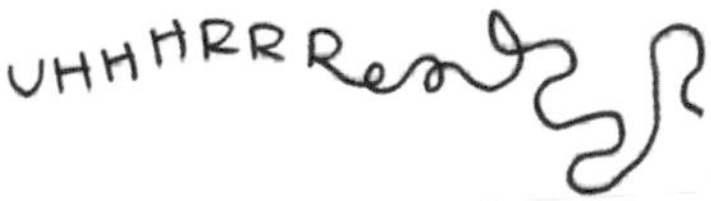
UHHHRRR

And that was it.

• • •

The emails I sent to exes did offer catharsis, certainly. But they weren't ~freeing~ in the way I told myself they were.

Because what were these emails besides Band-Aids to their egos, which I still felt compelled to protect even though we weren't together? That was the whole thing! I still thought they were good boys, and they had convinced me so thoroughly that my role was to uphold their goodness. It's why I "mutually" broke up with so many boys, which is to say I basically broke up with myself after they regurgitated half-formed feelings about where they were at, how they didn't want to hurt me but didn't know *what* they wanted.

I told myself these emails were "for me," a narrative I sloppily crafted when I would wake up in the middle of the night and realize that even after getting free of these boys who drained so many of my resources (energy, time, actual money, etc.), I was STILL BEING DRAINED. I was yelling into the void at people who were absolutely not ready to hear me and look at themselves in the ways I demanded.

* * *

It would be a better ending to this story if I said I never sent another one of these letters. That would be a lie. But Trash Cat* made me realize that what I actually wanted was a tangible way to measure the end of something, to find clarity amid a purposeful mess boys had left for me, withholding a finite ending, which allowed us to dwell in the murky "what if," the door back to each other always a bit ajar. I needed a clear-cut-decision moment: me or the trash. Though these boys didn't need closure, likely didn't want it, I did.

One of the friends whose home I arrived at soaking wet with the mysterious, terrified cat that fateful night told me that I was brave for sending the email. That it was an act of reclamation, a way to use my words to express a truth he didn't let me have. It was, in many ways, the start of the work I do now. My art is emotionally exhaustive, it's a tool, it's comedy, it's all of the things. But it's for me, it's for you—not them. Not him. By sending that email, I released a burden that wasn't really between me and this dude but something I had carried within myself. And the universe handed me back a cat.

Trash Cat, since renamed Louie, is now happily living in Upstate New York with one of the friends who was there on the night I received him. It turned out they had been looking to adopt a cat for months, and when I showed up sopping wet with a terrified one, it seemed like fate.

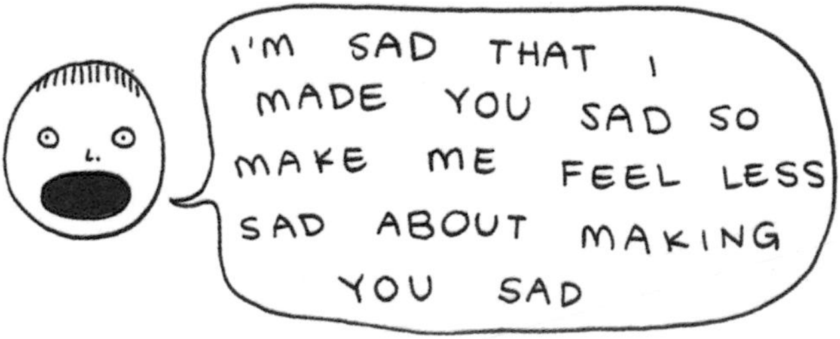
I'M SAD THAT I MADE YOU SAD SO MAKE ME FEEL LESS SAD ABOUT MAKING YOU SAD

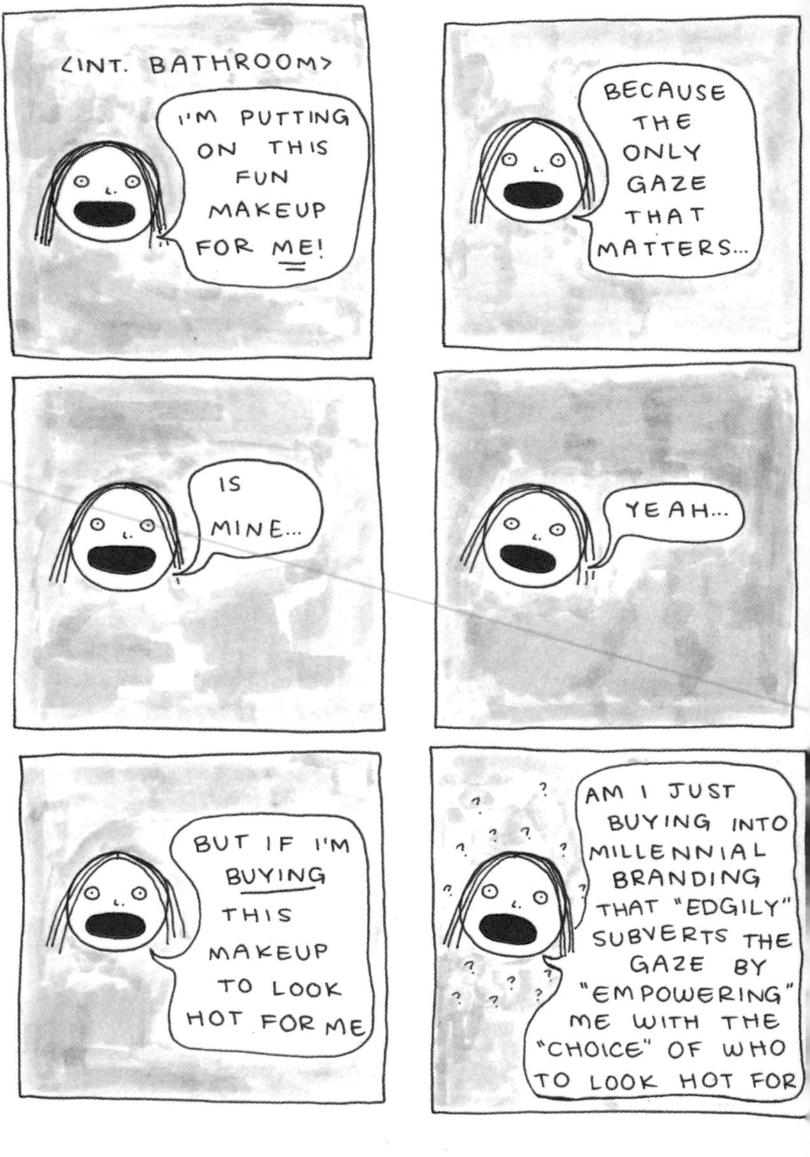
<INT. BATHROOM>
I'M PUTTING ON THIS FUN MAKEUP FOR ME!
BECAUSE THE ONLY GAZE THAT MATTERS...
IS MINE...
YEAH...
BUT IF I'M BUYING THIS MAKEUP TO LOOK HOT FOR ME
AM I JUST BUYING INTO MILLENNIAL BRANDING THAT "EDGILY" SUBVERTS THE GAZE BY "EMPOWERING" ME WITH THE "CHOICE" OF WHO TO LOOK HOT FOR

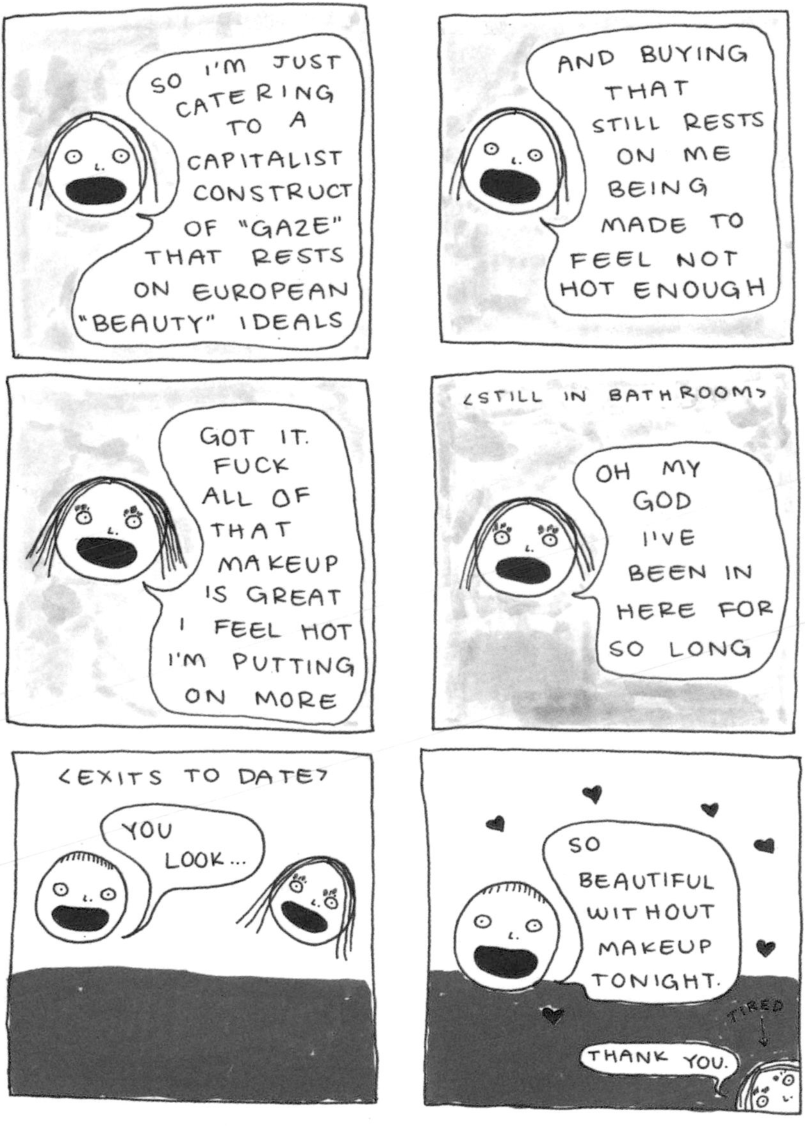
SO I'M JUST CATERING TO A CAPITALIST CONSTRUCT OF "GAZE" THAT RESTS ON EUROPEAN "BEAUTY" IDEALS
AND BUYING THAT STILL RESTS ON ME BEING MADE TO FEEL NOT HOT ENOUGH
GOT IT. FUCK ALL OF THAT MAKEUP IS GREAT I FEEL HOT I'M PUTTING ON MORE
<STILL IN BATHROOM>
OH MY GOD I'VE BEEN IN HERE FOR SO LONG
<EXITS TO DATE>
YOU LOOK...
SO BEAUTIFUL WITHOUT MAKEUP TONIGHT.
TIRED
THANK YOU.

THE VAMPIRE

THANK YOU FOR LETTING ME DRAIN YOU

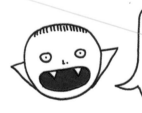

SO I COULD BECOME A CONVINCINGLY CAPABLE / SOCIALLY AWARE HUMAN!

AND MORE EASILY ATTRACT PEOPLE WHO WILL LIKE THE PERSON YOU MADE ME

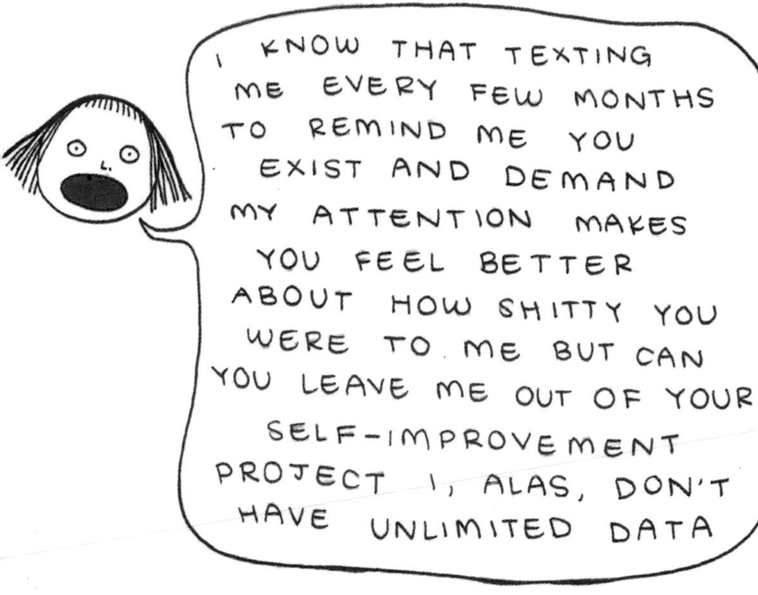
I KNOW THAT TEXTING ME EVERY FEW MONTHS TO REMIND ME YOU EXIST AND DEMAND MY ATTENTION MAKES YOU FEEL BETTER ABOUT HOW SHITTY YOU WERE TO ME BUT CAN YOU LEAVE ME OUT OF YOUR SELF-IMPROVEMENT PROJECT I, ALAS, DON'T HAVE UNLIMITED DATA

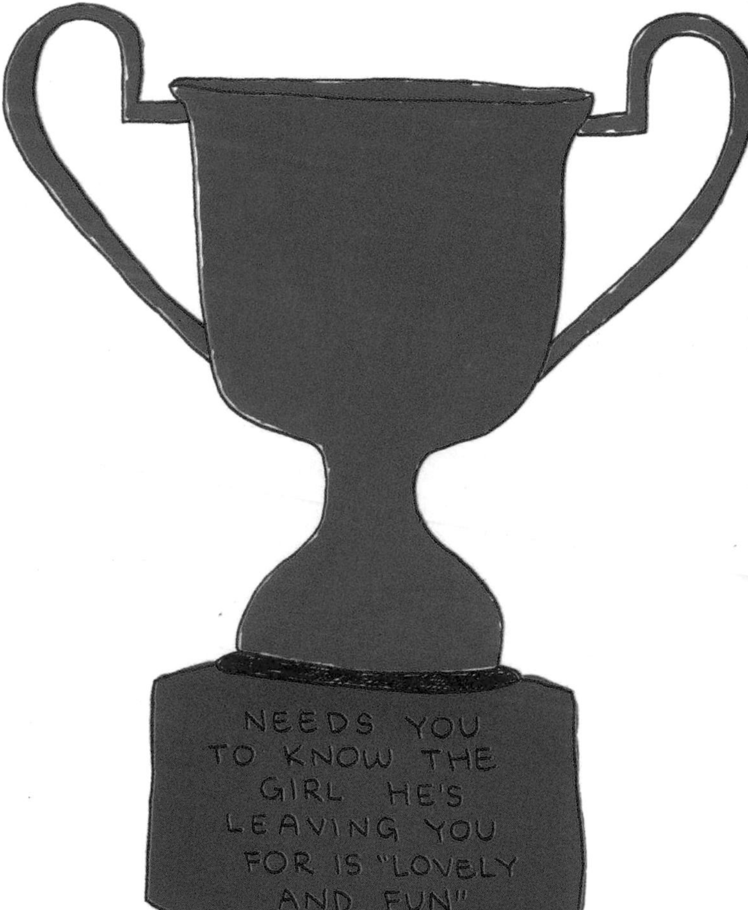
NEEDS YOU
TO KNOW THE
GIRL HE'S
LEAVING YOU
FOR IS "LOVELY
AND FUN"

WANT TO INVITE ME OVER, SPEND EMOTIONAL AND ACTUAL TIME ON GETTING READY FOR ME, GENTLY TIDY UP YOUR APARTMENT AND GRAB WINE, AND ANTICIPATE BEING FUCKED AT LEAST WELL, ALL SO I CAN SCROLL THROUGH MY TWITTER IN FRONT OF YOU FOR A WHILE?

I KNOW I FUCKED YOU OVER BUT WE TALKED ABOUT IT AND I'M RELATIVELY SORRY YOUR FEELINGS WERE HURT BUT WHAT I'M SAYING IS ISN'T IT ABOUT TIME YOU STARTED LIKING MY INSTAGRAM PHOTOS AGAIN???

CHAPTER 6

THE NOMENCLATURE OF THINGS

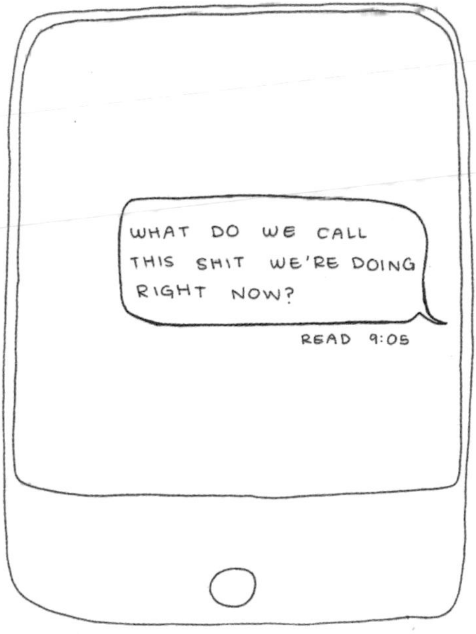

WHAT DO WE CALL THIS SHIT WE'RE DOING RIGHT NOW?
READ 9:05

THE NOMENCLATURE
OF THINGS
(OR, WHAT DO WE CALL THIS SHIT
WE'RE DOING RIGHT NOW)

Remember at the beginning of this book when I compared my wayward Tinder date to Icarus, waxen wings melting when he saw the walls of my room covered with awards?

Well, it wasn't the first time—I have seen such an Icarus before. I have seen him fall from grace after I asked what, apparently, is one of the scarier questions you can ask straight men you are fucking: *Can we check in about what we're doing, here, with each other?*

There's an argument to be made around how "casual relationships" today have become inherently more complicated, in practice and the language surrounding them, with the proliferation of online dating. We could blame modern dating problems on the gamification of dating via app, the seeming ubiquitousness of fuckable options, the flattening of people into consumable entities made even more apparent by the brand advertisements mixed right in with the people, one swipe separating your dream boyfriend and a Pop-Tart.

This idea is not *wrong*.

But it's also not what's happening here.

* * *

I decided to steal a different word to describe this sort of situation: liminal relationships. Relationships that exist torturously in the in-between.

Sometimes liminality is mutual. Other times it is born out of fear of commitment, out of what actually being with someone, being vulnerable and available, would mean. Sometimes it's a romance that starts with a built-in expiration date. Sometimes one person isn't ready for something serious but you hook up anyway, knowing eventually it'll just get more complicated than it already is.

The liminal relationship is often sexy and easy to romanticize *because* of the precariousness of its shape. How long can we get away with not defining this before we career headfirst into the mess we're making? Shall we try and see?

Some of these, as noted, are mutually agreed upon. But for years I was too generous around liminal relationships, seeing the best in them, the best in men, nodding along at being told "it just wasn't the right time" though they continued to date me, without a label, getting skittish when I even gestured toward a structure that would be more equitable, more fair, more communicative.

In retrospect, I see so many of these liminal relationships were by design: these casual things men refused to name were kept in linguistic purgatory to allow them, and only them, to reap the benefits of that in-between, of having it all without needing to show up. Upon reflection, I see so plainly what a grim equation it is: naming the casual would force them to be accountable, and definitively not-naming, releasing it from the liminal, would set me free, allow me to move on to someone not-them.

* * *

A weird side effect of the liminal is that communication goes out the window not just broadly but in small ways, too. By keeping the casual in linguistic/actual purgatory, he (I'm using this pronoun because it speaks to my experience, but this relationship fuckery applies to people of all genders) undermines the importance of clarifying the need-to-know things; for example, are you fucking other people? Is this a bedroom-only affair or should we see a movie? How often do you want to talk to each other? In refusing to delineate the edges of the casual, he makes it seem like anything you ask—*anything*—is not casual, which allows him to get away with everything he goddamn wants.

• • •

To be clear, none of these communication failures have to do with a relationship's label or lack thereof itself. It's just that: communication failure. People who are effectively hearing each other can call or not call what they're doing whatever they want and never even tiptoe near the liminal.

But perhaps unsurprisingly, as more and more nonconventional relationship models emerge or reemerge into prominence (a good thing!), modern good boys have really taken advantage of them—importantly, just the language, not the practice.

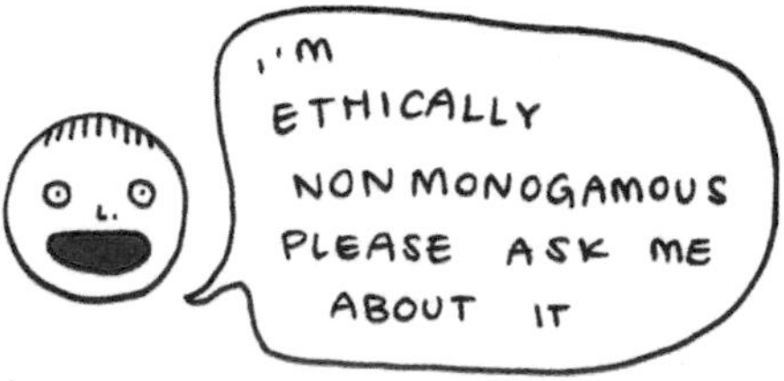
I'M ETHICALLY NON MONOGAMOUS PLEASE ASK ME ABOUT IT

There are now ample terms that good boys seem to think can be slapped onto a relationship and voilà! Now you are that. Like one of those sticky hands you get for a quarter at a bowling alley, I watched boys fling around the term "open relationship" to see where it stuck. What better way to slither around the liminal than to co-opt the language of a relationship model that, in these boys' minds, apparently allows you to do whatever you want, fuck whoever you want without reproach?

In one such liminal relationship I had years ago, I was made to feel that my need for further structure, for a "normative" label, was the problem, rather than the fact that we weren't in a real open relationship, merely calling it that. I didn't *want* to be someone for whom labels mattered, but I knew that this thing? It was the liminal dressed in "ethically nonmonogamous" clothing. These boys seemed to think that if they swung the linguistic sticky hand at "open," and it stuck, that was it, that was enough. When I tried, in vain, to explain that functional nonmonogamous partnerships, like any, take SO MUCH FUCKING WORK AND LITERAL PLANNING, they seemed incredulous.

I'm done with liminals, swearing off them forever. I've traversed this shadow realm for too long, and I advise you to swear off them, too. This doesn't mean "don't casually date." It just means: don't casually date people who refuse to communicate about the casual. Don't allow people to falsely equate communication and clarity with seriousness. It's a requirement. Don't settle for less.

I REALLY, REALLY TOLERATE YOU
OMG THANK YOU! I REALLY TOLERATE YOU TOO
LET'S "DATE" UNTIL WE MEET PEOPLE WE LIKE MORE?
YES!
SHE SAID YES!

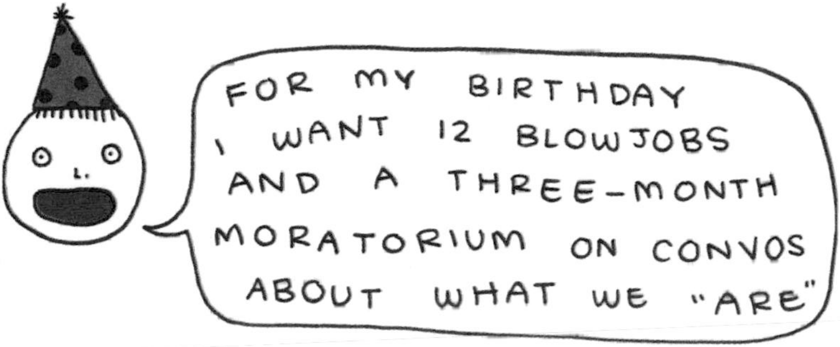

FOR MY BIRTHDAY
I WANT 12 BLOWJOBS
AND A THREE-MONTH
MORATORIUM ON CONVOS
ABOUT WHAT WE "ARE"

SORRY IF ME REACHING OUT FOR NO REASON AT ALL FUCKS YOU UP FOR WEEKS IT'S JUST YOU POSTED A PICTURE OF YOU WEARING EYE MAKEUP THAT INDICATED YOU WERE GOING OUT AND IT REMINDED ME THAT YOU WERE MOVING ON SO I THOUGHT I'D POP IN TO MAKE THAT HARDER

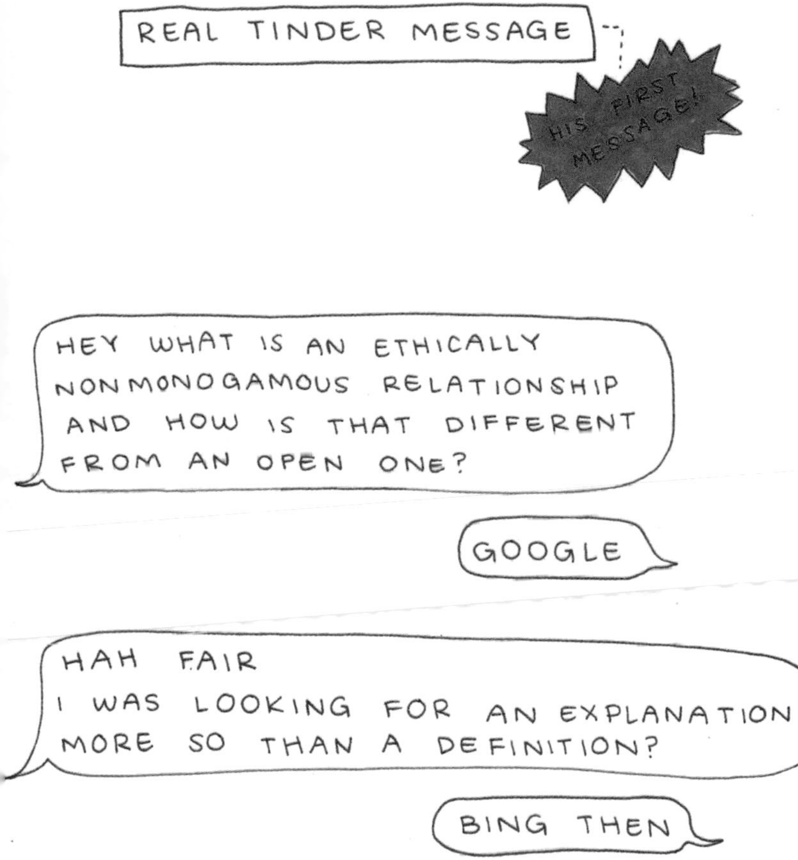
REAL TINDER MESSAGE
HIS FIRST MESSAGE!
HEY WHAT IS AN ETHICALLY NONMONOGAMOUS RELATIONSHIP AND HOW IS THAT DIFFERENT FROM AN OPEN ONE?
GOOGLE
HAH FAIR
I WAS LOOKING FOR AN EXPLANATION MORE SO THAN A DEFINITION?
BING THEN

TELLS YOU
HE LIKES YOU!
BUT WANTS TO CLARIFY
THAT HE'S HAPPY IN THIS
LIMINAL, DATING - BUT -NOT-
DATING THING AND HE
ISN'T INTERESTED IN KIDS
OR PERSONALIZED WEDDING
VOWS OR A JOINT CHECK-
ING ACCOUNT SO DON'T GET
THE WRONG IDEA, OKAY?

I WENT ON A DATE WITH SOMEONE AND REALIZED IT WILL TAKE A WHILE TO TEACH SOMEONE HOW TO FEEL MY FEELINGS FOR ME AND I DON'T REALLY HAVE THE ENERGY SO WANT TO GET BACK TOGETHER?

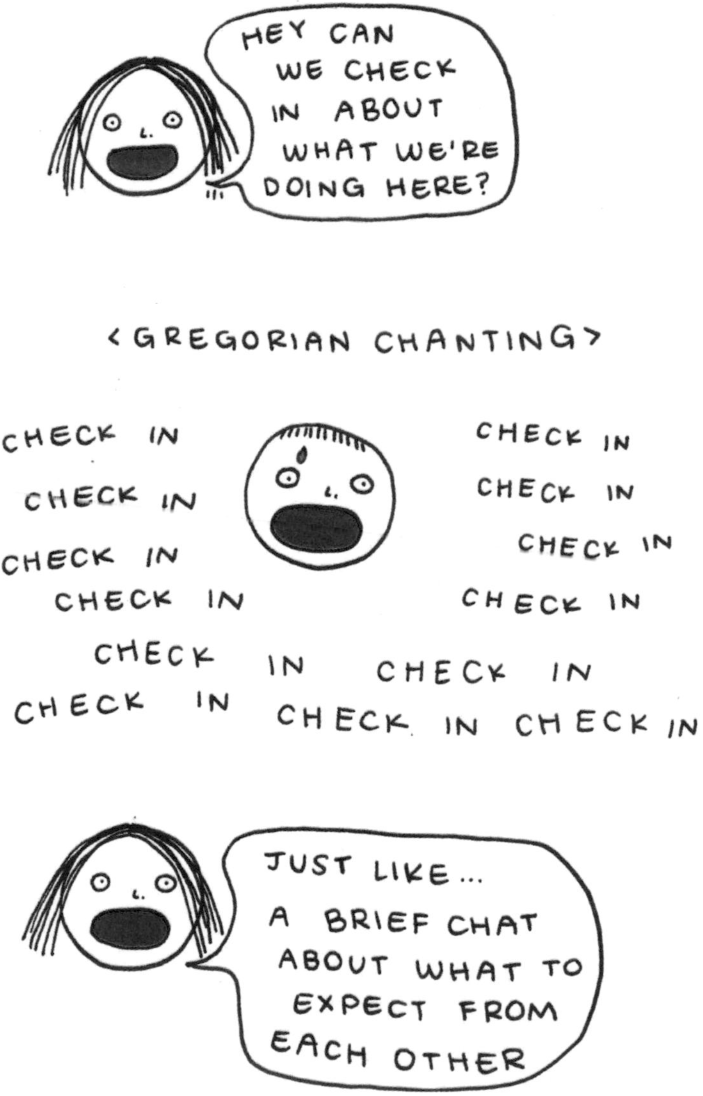
HEY CAN WE CHECK IN ABOUT WHAT WE'RE DOING HERE?
<GREGORIAN CHANTING>
CHECK IN CHECK IN CHECK IN CHECK IN CHECK IN CHECK IN CHECK IN CHECK IN CHECK IN CHECK IN CHECK IN CHECK IN CHECK IN
JUST LIKE... A BRIEF CHAT ABOUT WHAT TO EXPECT FROM EACH OTHER

<CHANTING CONTINUES>

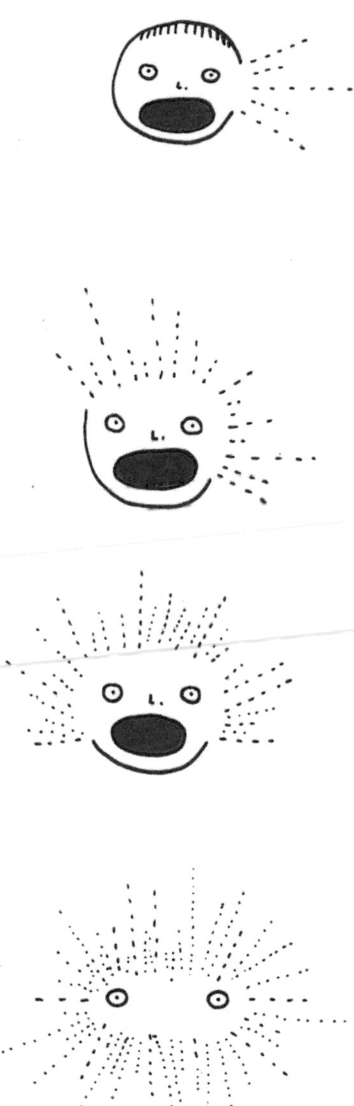

AND/OR GESTURES BROADLY AT

<FLICKS ^ YOUR GENITALIA>

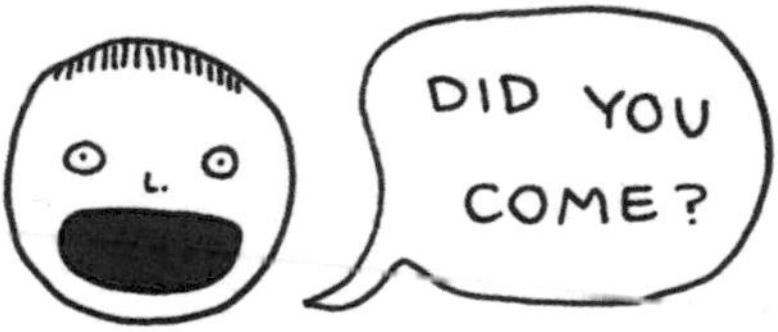
DID YOU COME?

MOMENTS AFTER AN APOCALYPTIC WORLD EVENT INTERRUPTED SEX

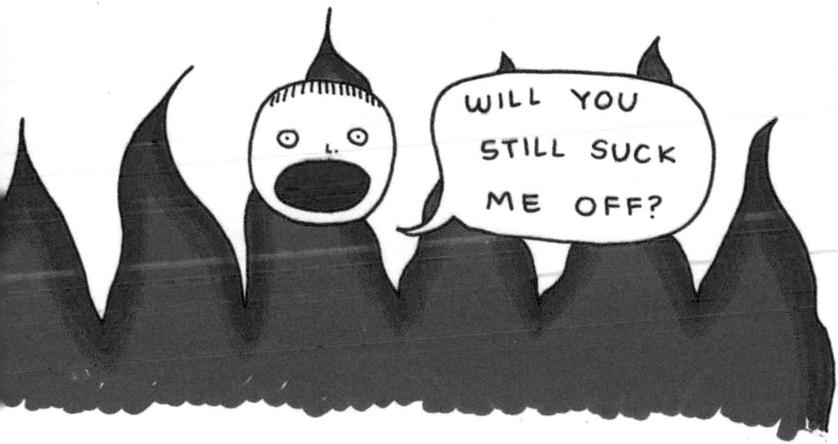
WILL YOU STILL SUCK ME OFF?

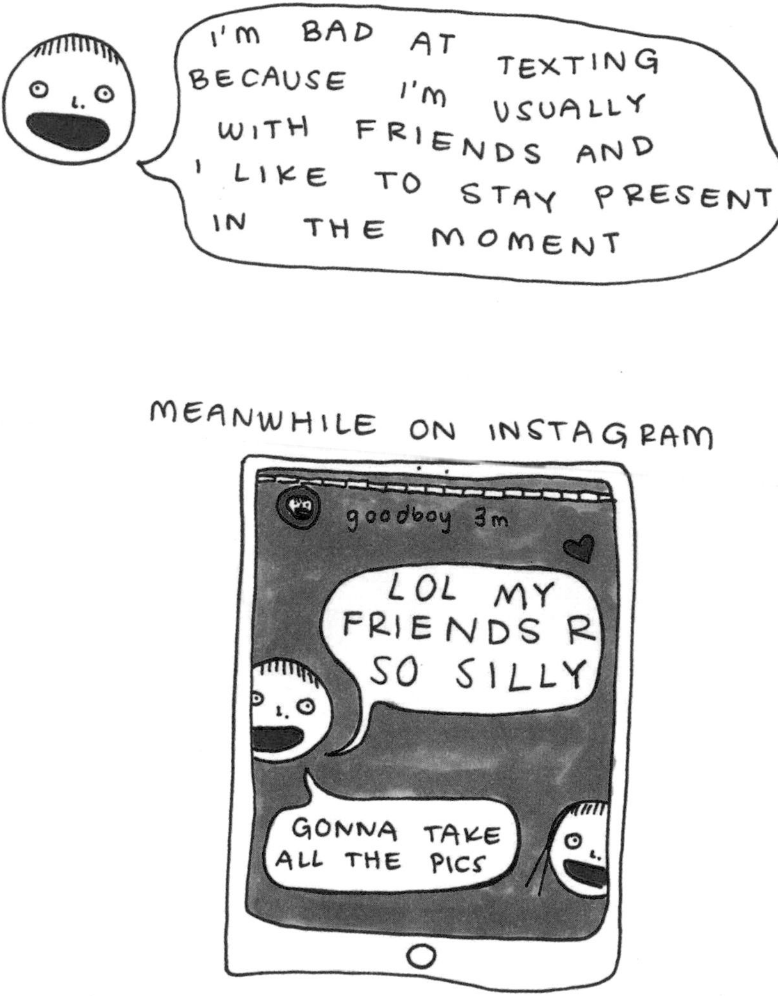
I'M BAD AT TEXTING BECAUSE I'M USUALLY WITH FRIENDS AND I LIKE TO STAY PRESENT IN THE MOMENT
MEANWHILE ON INSTAGRAM
goodboy 3m
LOL MY FRIENDS R SO SILLY
GONNA TAKE ALL THE PICS

HASN'T INTRODUCED YOU, THEIR PARTNER, AS "MY FRIEND" IN A WHILE!

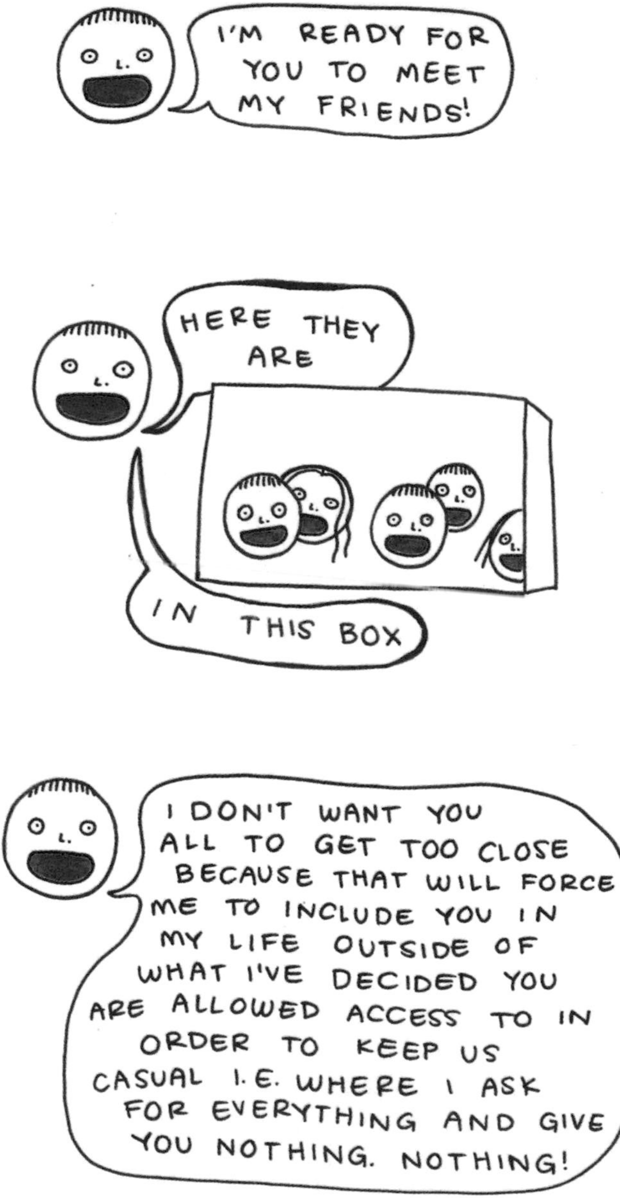
I'M READY FOR YOU TO MEET MY FRIENDS!
HERE THEY ARE
IN THIS BOX
I DON'T WANT YOU ALL TO GET TOO CLOSE BECAUSE THAT WILL FORCE ME TO INCLUDE YOU IN MY LIFE OUTSIDE OF WHAT I'VE DECIDED YOU ARE ALLOWED ACCESS TO IN ORDER TO KEEP US CASUAL I.E. WHERE I ASK FOR EVERYTHING AND GIVE YOU NOTHING. NOTHING!

YE OLDE LIMINAL RELATIONSHIP

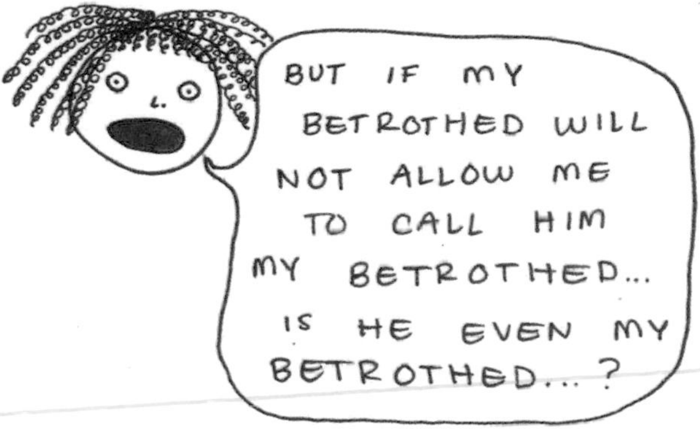

NO YOU ARE BASICALLY MY GIRLFRIEND I JUST THINK LABELS ARE PART OF THE HETERONORMATIVE BINARY AND NOMENCLATURE-OBSESSED SOCIETAL CLUSTERFUCK

A GOOD BOY'S JOURNEY
OH I FEEL SO SAD I HURT HER SEEING HER SAD MAKES ME FEEL LIKE A BAD BOY.
EVEN THOUGH IT'S NEARLY IMPOSSIBLE BECAUSE I WANT TO BE ACKNOWLEDGED AND PRAISED FOR MATURELY GIVING YOU SPACE LIKE YOU ASKED FOR, I WILL GIVE YOU THE SPACE YOU NEED.
OK ON SECOND THOUGHT I WANT TO NORMALIZE THINGS SO I FEEL OKAY / TEMPORARILY FORGET THAT I MADE THIS HAPPEN SO I'M GONNA SEND YOU SOME MEMES REAL FAST
ACTUALLY THAT'S UNFAIR OF ME. YOU DO YOU. I'LL TEXT YOU WHEN YOU LEAST WANT IT IN A FEW MONTHS. ALSO I WON'T RESPOND IF YOU TEXT ME BECAUSE I'M FUCKING A HOT GIRL AND THINGS ARE GOING REALLY WELL!
SHE DIDN'T STIMULATE MY MIND LIKE YOU DID SO I'M GONNA KEEP FUCKING HER AND ALSO SEEK OUT YOUR MIND
STAY TUNED FOR: A HEARTFELT DRUNK TEXT HE'LL TAKE NO ACCOUNTABILITY FOR MORNING AFTER!

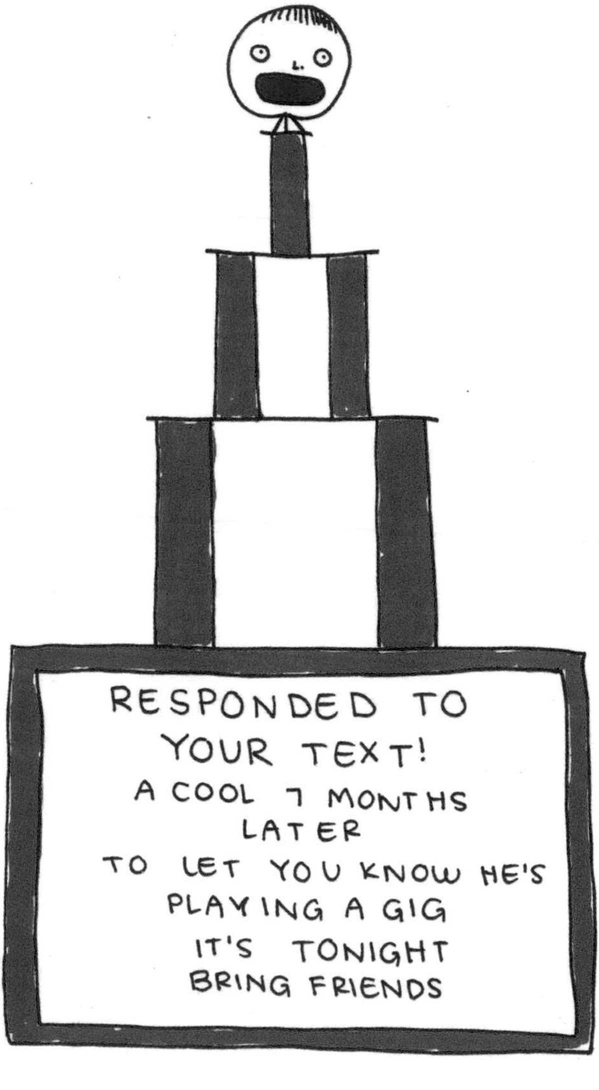
RESPONDED TO
YOUR TEXT!
A COOL 7 MONTHS
LATER
TO LET YOU KNOW HE'S
PLAYING A GIG
IT'S TONIGHT
BRING FRIENDS

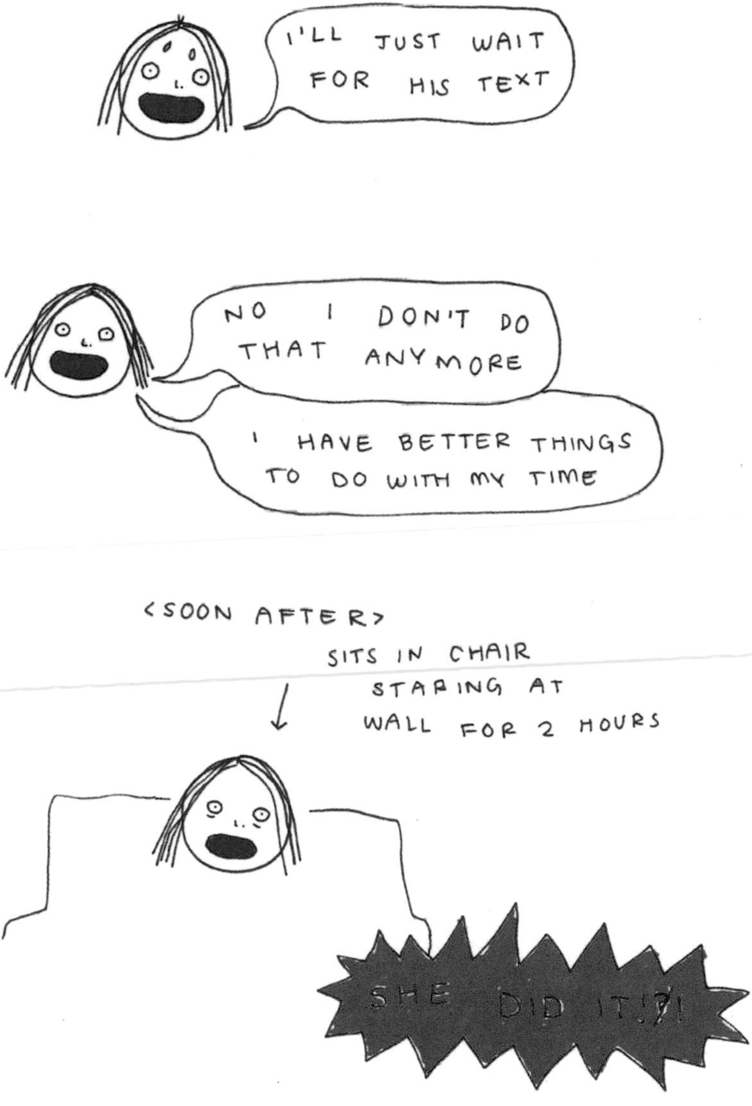
I'LL JUST WAIT FOR HIS TEXT
NO I DON'T DO THAT ANYMORE
I HAVE BETTER THINGS TO DO WITH MY TIME
<SOON AFTER>
SITS IN CHAIR STARING AT WALL FOR 2 HOURS
SHE DID IT!?!

I'M JUST...
NOT READY...
FOR YOUR FULL NAME IN MY CONTACTS

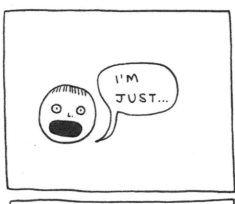

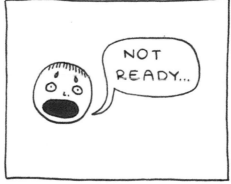

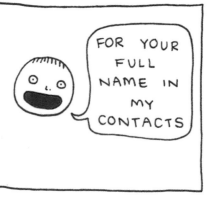

CHAPTER 7

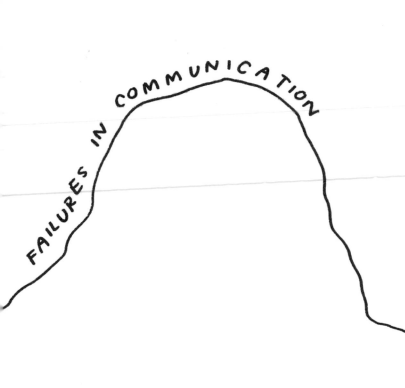

FAILURES IN COMMUNICATION

FAILURES IN COMMUNICATION

(OR, THE MASHED-POTATO MOUNTAIN FROM CLOSE ENCOUNTERS OF THE THIRD KIND)

One of my favorite movies growing up was *Close Encounters of the Third Kind*. This isn't why I loved it, but one scene has really stayed with me: when Richard Dreyfuss, after seeing an alien spaceship hover across the night sky, impulsively sculpts a mashed-potato mountain, not knowing what it is exactly he's crafted.

It turns out everyone who saw the spaceships has started sculpting the same shape—it's a location; they don't know that yet—because, basically, they don't have the words to describe what they know. They witnessed something and were imbued with knowledge that was indescribable. So they throw away language, not helpful here, and grasp at other ways to describe what words cannot. They start getting creative. Including, but not limited to, building the mashed-potato mountain.

It's a great scene. The character frantically scoops mashed potatoes into a mound of such size that it makes one wonder why this family had so many mashed potatoes to begin with, and realize how the crew must have really hated this day on set, and how it was someone's job to make this many mashed potatoes for the movie, and how I hope they told that story to people afterward in a knowing, self-righteous sort of way. Like: *Yes, I was the mashed-potato man in* Close Encounters of the Third Kind.

I keep returning to this scene because it's hilarious, but also because I love metaphors and this is an apt one, and extremely meta at that. It feels like a good descriptor for failures in communication—what it is to articulate experiences you yourself may not understand or have the words for, or don't have the words for yet, but nevertheless know to be real.

*   *   *

Whether or not we try to "accurately" capture our experiences, with words or art or tweets, we are offloading all the time. To Google, to social media. The ways we try, intentionally and not, to immortalize ourselves by segmenting a piece of us away in others or on the web. Very horcrux. Extremely horcrux.

What about the stories we offload to others? The ones we leave behind in people?

I have become (and still am) fixated on the sheer fact that other people, exes mainly, carry different narratives of our shared time together than I do. I imagine theirs are so forgiving of themselves, as mine are forgiving of me. Perhaps, I imagine, they still hold themselves aloft with the idea that they are "a good guy"—it's likely why, to some extent, I spend so long after breakups ruminating on what was and then promptly offloading my own experiences of it *back* to them. My This Is How You Wronged Me emails were not just about releasing a burden but about putting in writing—this, I was good at—a concrete reflection of what was.

*   *   *

It's perhaps unsurprising that years ago I became fixated on tangible offloading—the kind that I could, ever so slightly, separate from myself and call catharsis so as to not look too closely at how I dwelled, how I obsessed, with the stories other people told themselves about me.

I watched movies and TV shows and read stories about people offloading things to robots, to machines, which is, like, so much of media. All the sci-fi. I watched a video (repeatedly) of Whoopi Goldberg talking to Bina48, an extremely scary-I-mean-cool robot created by a team under Martine Rothblatt, an entrepreneur and inventor who modeled the robot on the real face, memory, and words of her embodied and still-alive wife, ALSO NAMED BINA.

I was fascinated with the impossibility of these projects, both imagined and real, that aim to store everything, even as we're running out of space to do so. (I saw a *Nat Geo* article once about how even DNA is being used for data storage now.) It became a question for me much like what species we should save in the face of climate change or what would be on the next Voyager Golden Record: What is important? What gets stored? What gets left behind? At some point someone (you already know who) has to choose.

*   *   *

So much of my work, at its core, is about the things words fail to describe. It's about my own impulse to cement my version of the story in ink, words, art. It's about reconciling the stories we've been told, the ones we tell each other, and the ones people take away.

This project is selfish. It's also incomplete. I started it because I was ruminating over the stories I knew had been twisted and bent by the men I made myself small for. I started it because I realized my attempts to correct the record of others' stories about me were both futile and impossible. Why did I need these men to think a specific way about me? Wasn't I just stepping into my own ironic trap, forever trying to prove to them—and myself—that though I was fallible, at least things were of my own design?

*   *   *

Which makes it clear, to me, that what should be left behind in *this* very text are not just my words, but yours, too. I don't have the words for experiences that aren't my own. There are gaps in the story only you can fill, as you'll see in the ACTIVITY SECTION COMING RIGHT UP AFTER THIS CHAPTER for you to offload.

When did we start pretending anything is done, anything is total, anything is complete? This is a moving, shifting, living text, as every text is. I'm writing this months before the book will come out, in a world that is increasingly chaotic, with an acute sense of how, yeah, we might all be apocalyptic rubble really soon. In fact, that would be great. Please end us!

If I can deem my words worthy of being found among rubble, please believe that yours are worthy, too, regardless of what your words sound like, regardless of whether they are words at all. Make mashed-potato mountains.

I hope that for one person, or perhaps two, I've created a framework that you can use as a springboard to name something that has eluded you as it has eaten up your valuable mental space, and time, and energy. Use this—twist it and bend it to your will. Pile on those potatoes, hopefully an absurd amount (where did they come from?!), and trust that the Important part isn't what you make, how beautiful it is, how high the potatoes stack, but the process of flailing toward meaning, of giving shape to what you've been told, and told yourself, doesn't matter. Make something, even if only decipherable between you and yourself. Take a little bit of the time you've unknowingly or knowingly spent awarding good boys for their minuscule deeds, and reward yourself for being enough.

You deserve to tell your story, and you deserve to laugh. I hope I've helped a little bit.

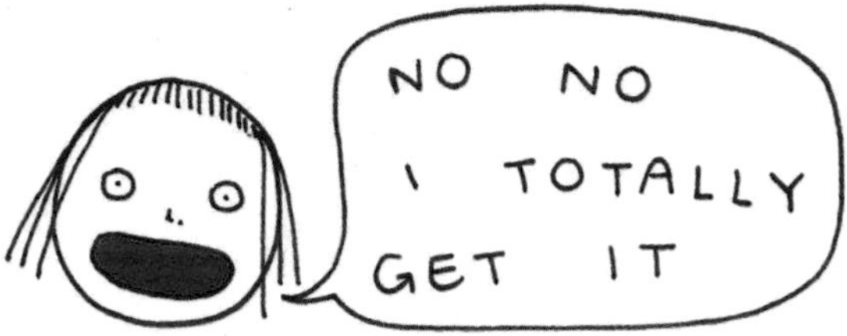
NO NO I TOTALLY GET IT

BUT IN TRUTH, SHE DID <u>NOT</u> "GET IT" AND WAS MERELY TRYING TO END THE CONVERSATION

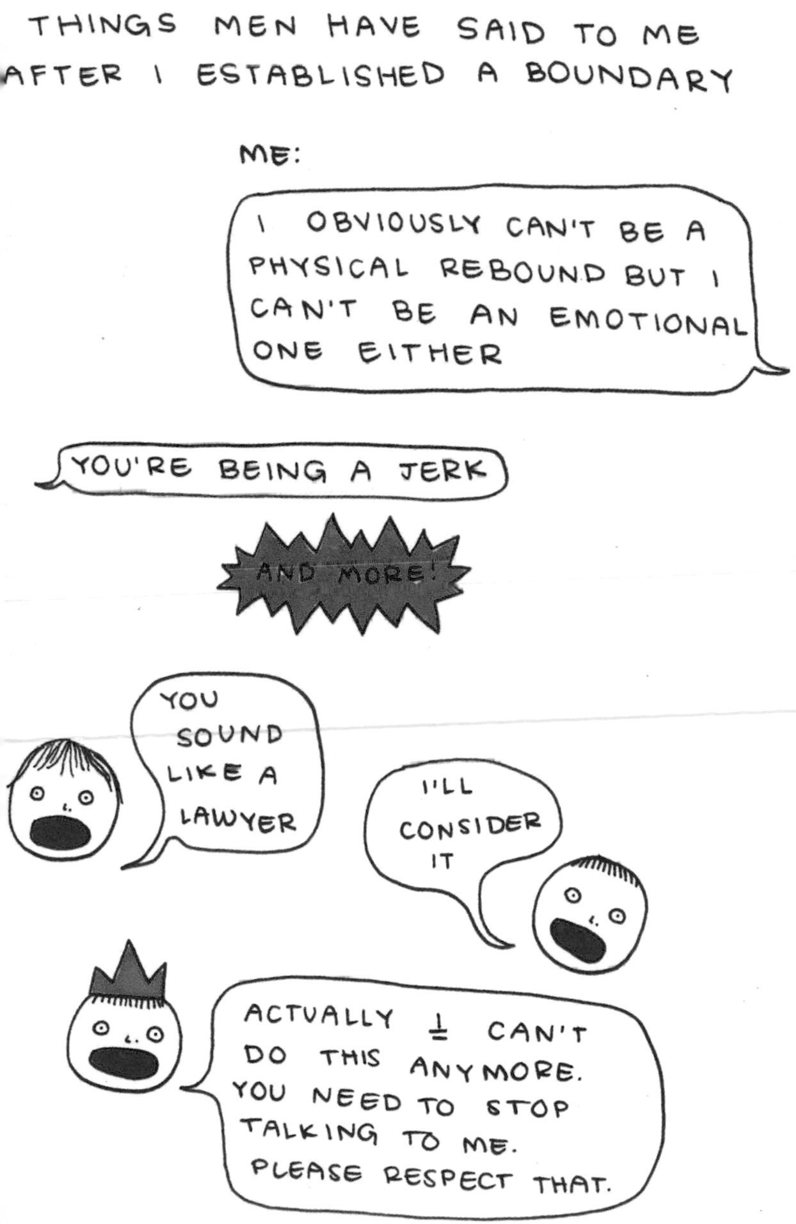
THINGS MEN HAVE SAID TO ME AFTER I ESTABLISHED A BOUNDARY
ME:
I OBVIOUSLY CAN'T BE A PHYSICAL REBOUND BUT I CAN'T BE AN EMOTIONAL ONE EITHER
YOU'RE BEING A JERK
AND MORE!
YOU SOUND LIKE A LAWYER
I'LL CONSIDER IT
ACTUALLY I CAN'T DO THIS ANYMORE. YOU NEED TO STOP TALKING TO ME. PLEASE RESPECT THAT.

A SONG I SING:

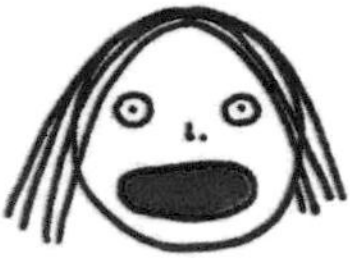

IT'S SOOOOO HARD TO TELL IF MEN ARE BEING CREEPY OR NICE

REFRAIN:

AND IF "NICE" WHAAAAT DOES IT MEAN IS THIS "NICE TO GET INTO YOUR BED" OR NICE UNTIL JUST AFTER SEX OR NICE BECAUSE PEOPLE CAN BE NICEEEEE

ARCHETYPAL DUDE YOU SEE ON TINDER # 158

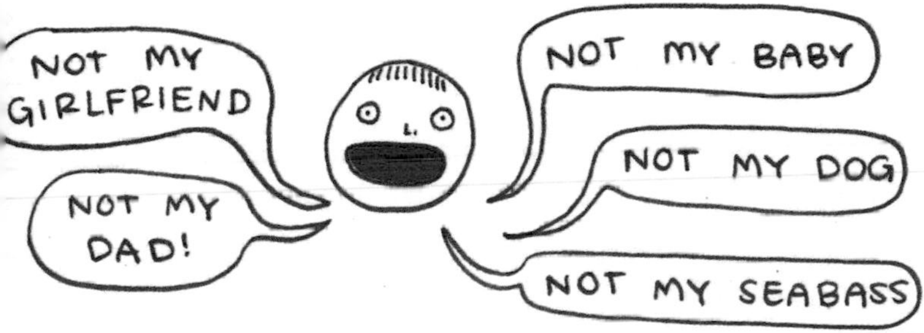
NOT MY GIRLFRIEND
NOT MY DAD!
NOT MY BABY
NOT MY DOG
NOT MY SEABASS

THE DUDE WHO DIDN'T HAVE... ANY? PICTURES OF HIM WITHOUT A THING TO DISCLAIM

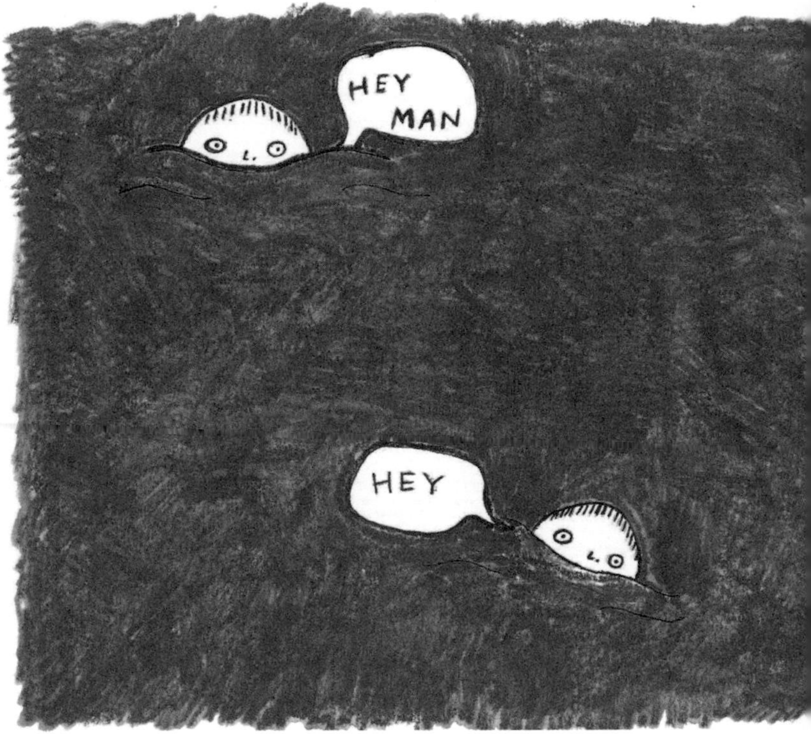
HEY MAN
HEY

A LIFETIME SPENT SUPPRESSING EMOTIONS (AND TEARS) FINALLY CAUGHT UP TO SAL AND SAUL

YE OLDE "LEFT ON READ"

* RAVEN? I DON'T KNOW. BLAME SCI/FI + HIGH FANTASY.

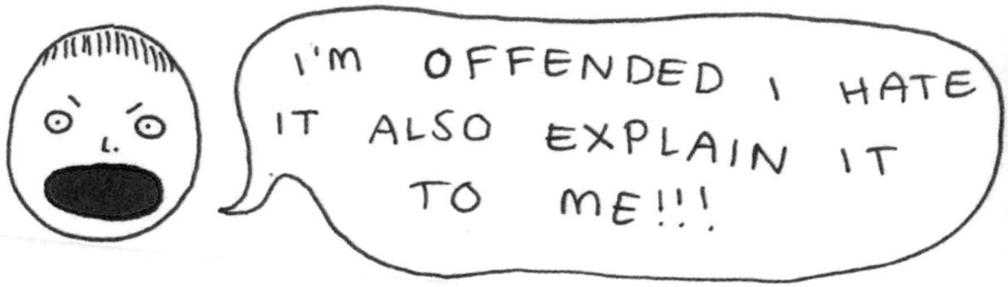
I'M OFFENDED I HATE IT ALSO EXPLAIN IT TO ME!!!

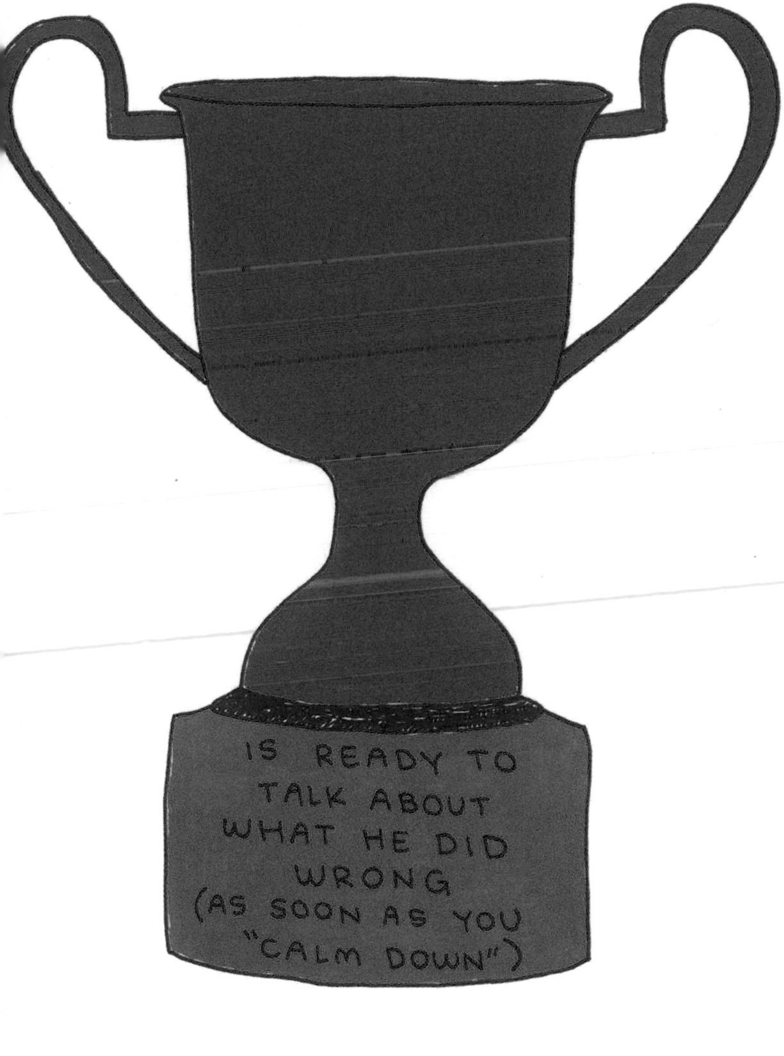
IS READY TO
TALK ABOUT
WHAT HE DID
WRONG
(AS SOON AS YOU
"CALM DOWN")

ARCHETYPAL DUDE YOU SEE ON TINDER # 635

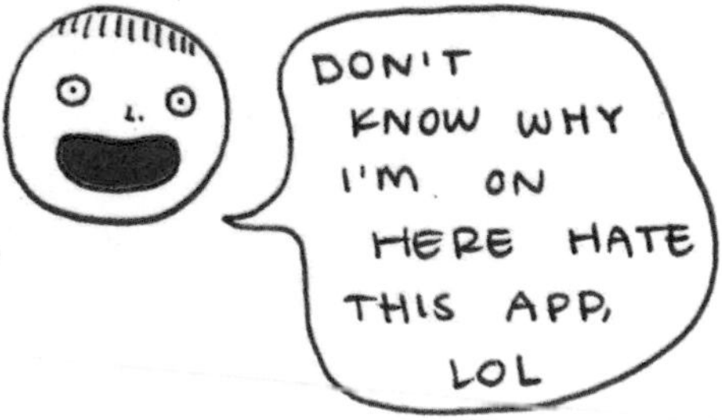
DON'T KNOW WHY I'M ON HERE HATE THIS APP, LOL

GUY WHO THINKS HE'S UNIQUE IN HIS APATHY FOR ONLINE DATING AND KINDLY GIFTS YOU THE BURDEN OF CARRYING THE ENTIRE CONVERSATION

TRUE OR FALSE:

I LOVE YOU OH MY GOD I MEANT GOOD NIGHT

DID I TELL THE FIRST
BOY I MADE OUT WITH
THAT I LOVED HIM MERE
SECONDS AFTER THE SMOOCH
TURN PAGE OVER FOR ANSWER

I DID IT I DID THE THING I REALLY DID

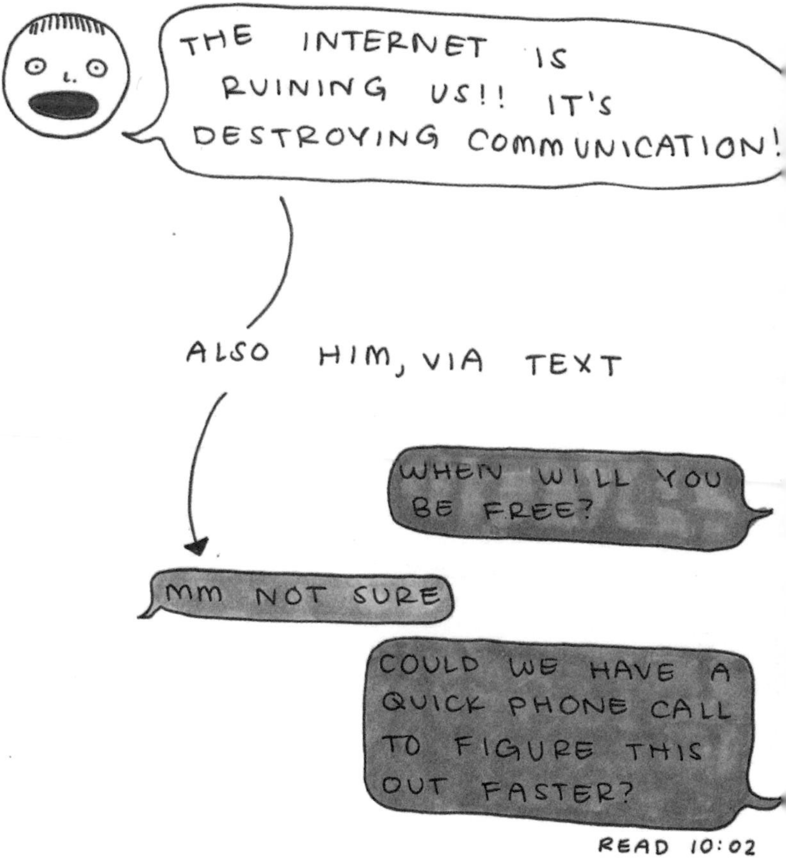
THE INTERNET IS RUINING US!! IT'S DESTROYING COMMUNICATION!
ALSO HIM, VIA TEXT
WHEN WILL YOU BE FREE?
MM NOT SURE
COULD WE HAVE A QUICK PHONE CALL TO FIGURE THIS OUT FASTER?
READ 10:02

GOOD BOYS HAVE AN AVERSION
TO PHONE CALLS?

YES.

BECAUSE VIA PHONE YOU CANNOT
1) LEAVE ON READ
2) RESPOND IN 5 DAYS
CAUSE YOU'RE "BAD AT TEXTING"

PHONE CALLS HOLD YOU MORE
ACCOUNTABLE, WHICH IS PERHAPS
WHY GOOD BOYS DETEST THEM SO MUCH.

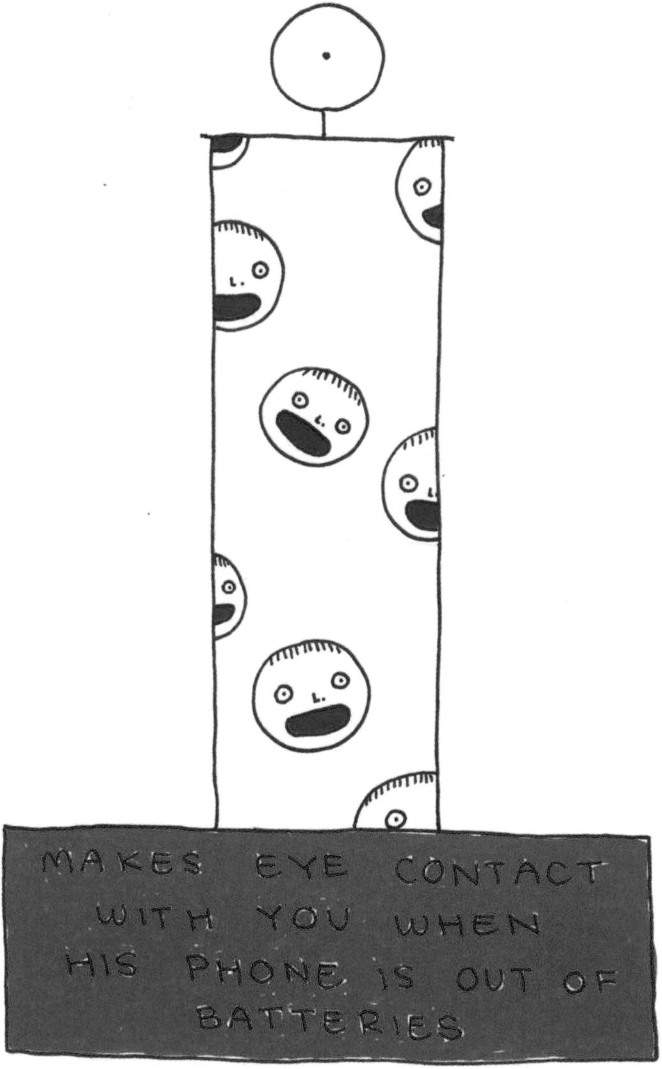
MAKES EYE CONTACT WITH YOU WHEN HIS PHONE IS OUT OF BATTERIES

JOHN MAYER'S HOT TAKE
(ADAPTED FROM REAL QUOTE)

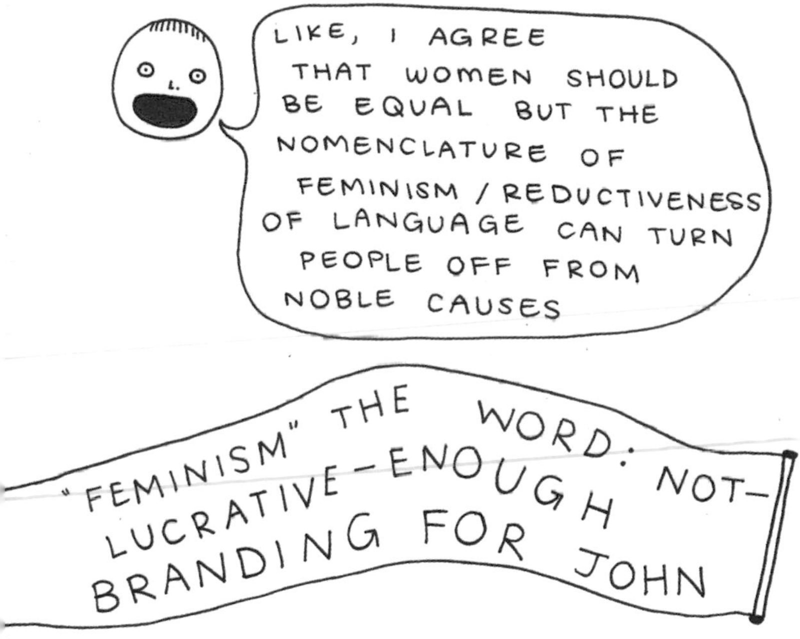

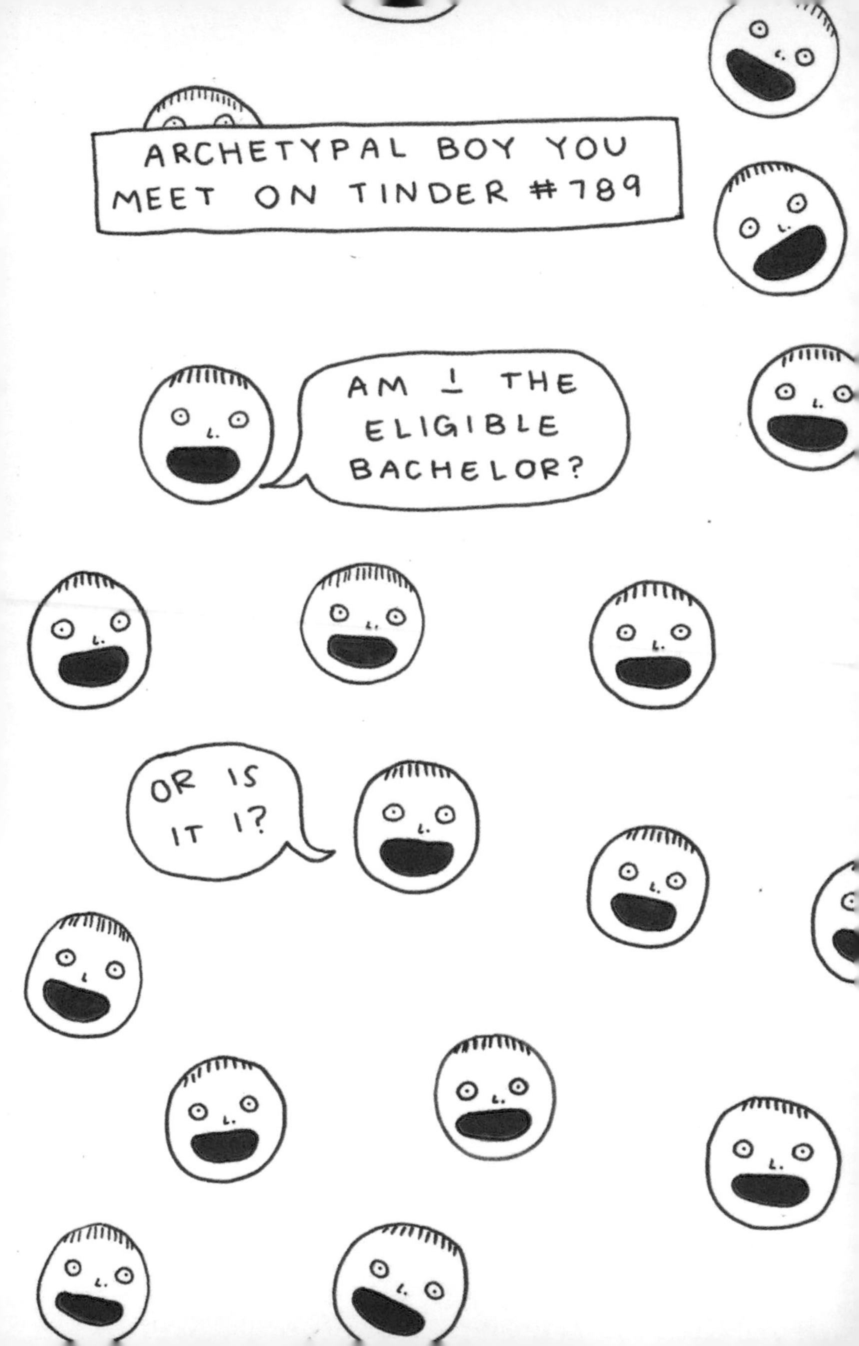
ARCHETYPAL BOY YOU MEET ON TINDER #789
AM I THE ELIGIBLE BACHELOR?
OR IS IT I?

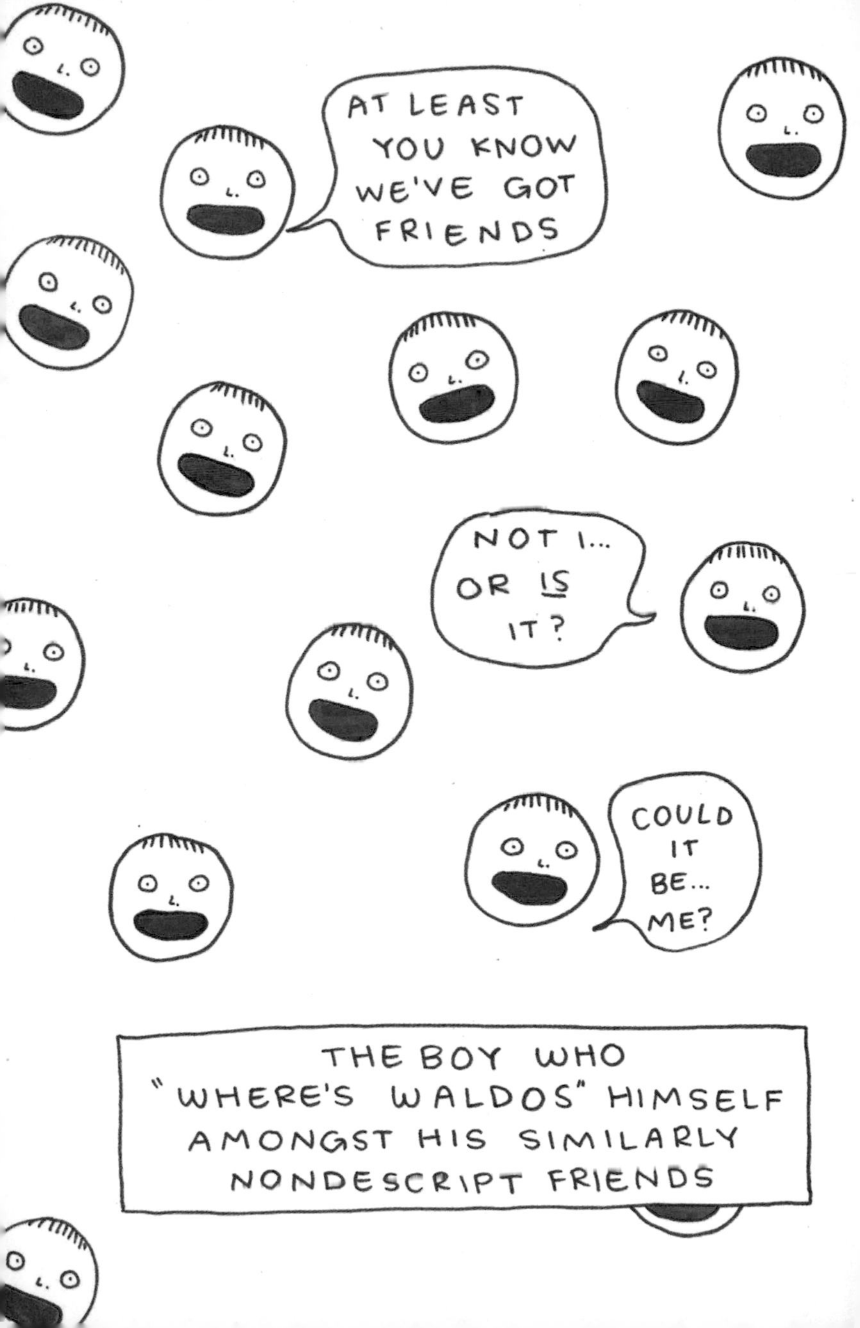

AT LEAST YOU KNOW WE'VE GOT FRIENDS
NOT I... OR IS IT?
COULD IT BE... ME?
THE BOY WHO "WHERE'S WALDOS" HIMSELF AMONGST HIS SIMILARLY NONDESCRIPT FRIENDS

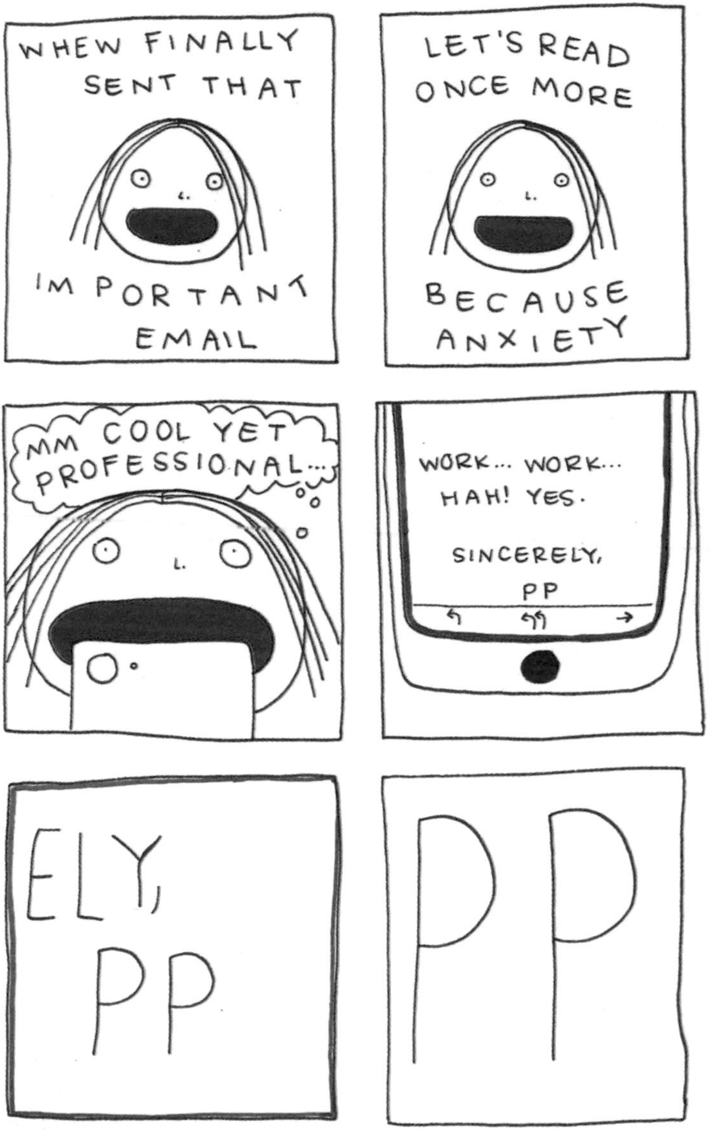
WHEW FINALLY SENT THAT
IMPORTANT EMAIL
LET'S READ ONCE MORE
BECAUSE ANXIETY
MM COOL YET PROFESSIONAL...
WORK... WORK...
HAH! YES.
SINCERELY,
PP
ELY,
PP
PP

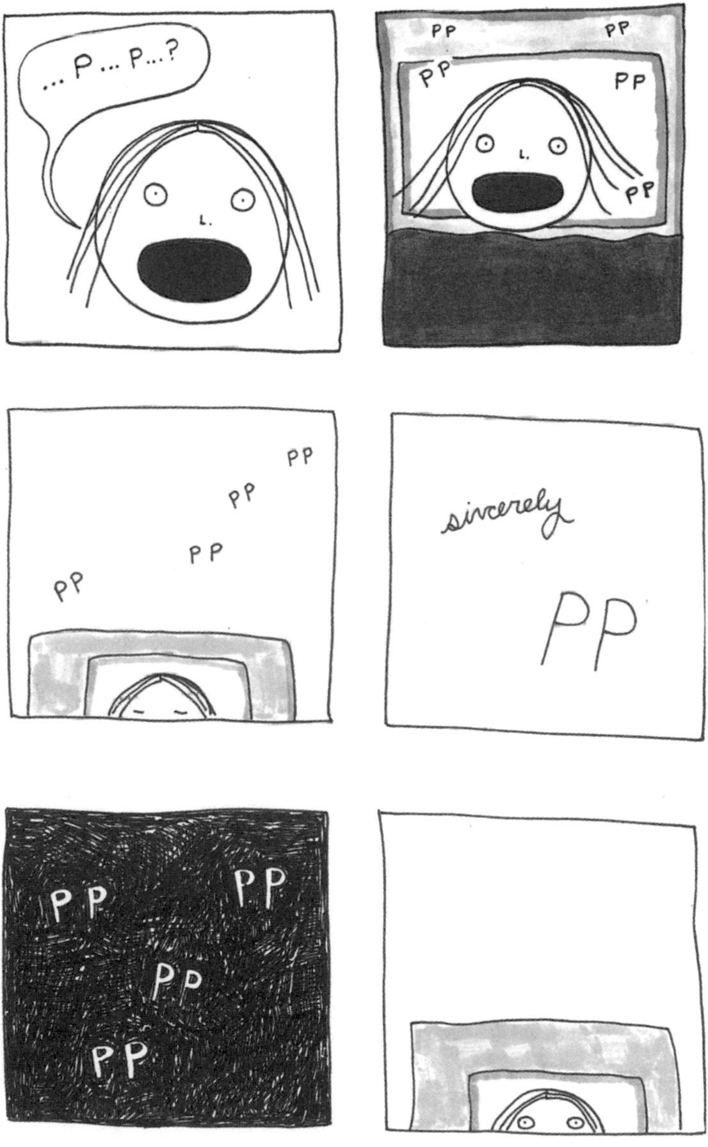
... P ... P ...?
PP
PP
PP
PP
PP
PP
PP
PP
PP
sincerely
PP
PP
PP
PP
PP

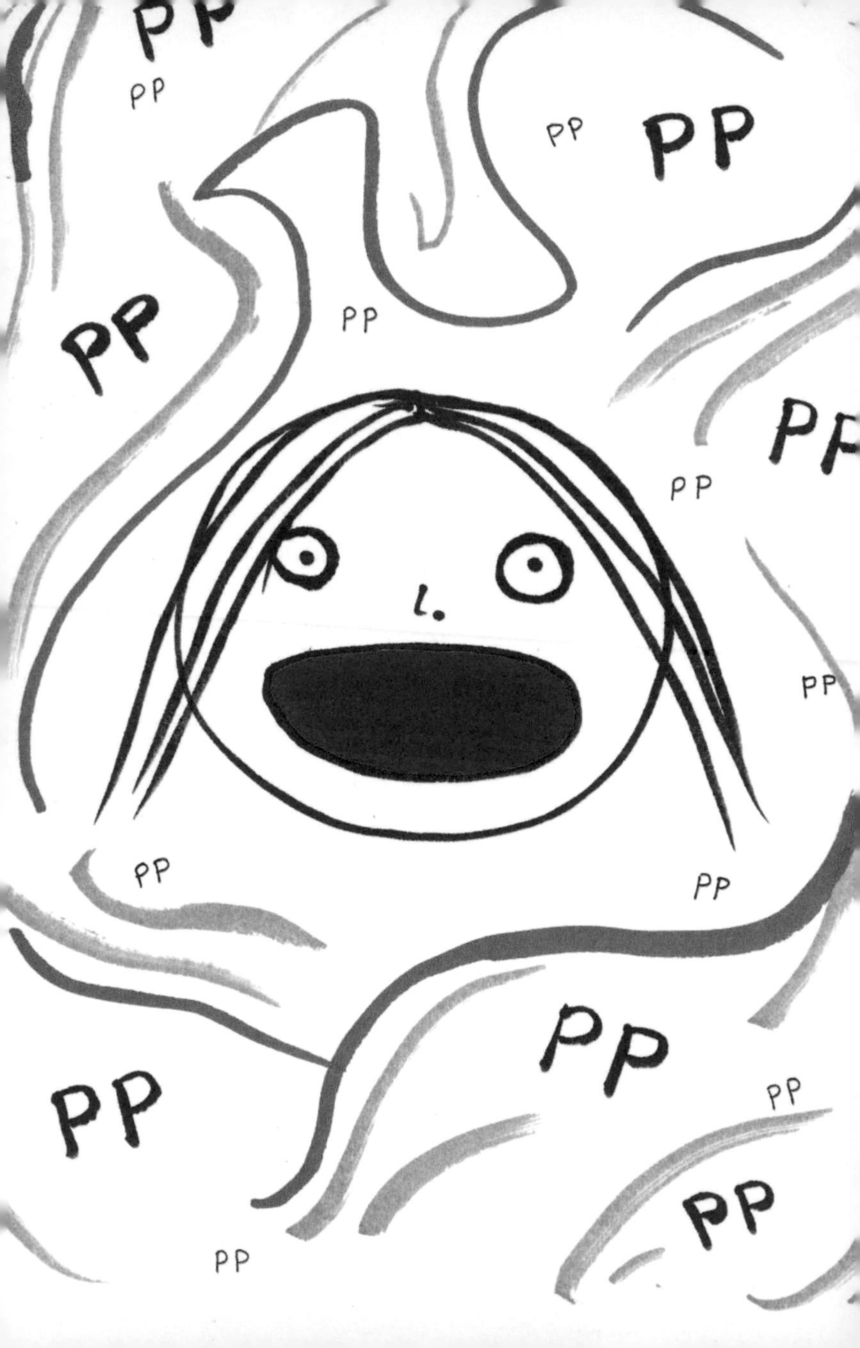
pp
pp
PP
PP
pp
pp
pp
pp
pp
PP
PP
pp
PP
pp

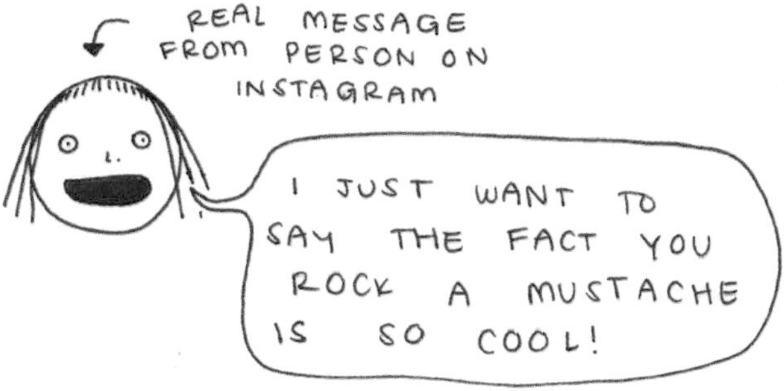
REAL MESSAGE FROM PERSON ON INSTAGRAM
I JUST WANT TO SAY THE FACT YOU ROCK A MUSTACHE IS SO COOL!

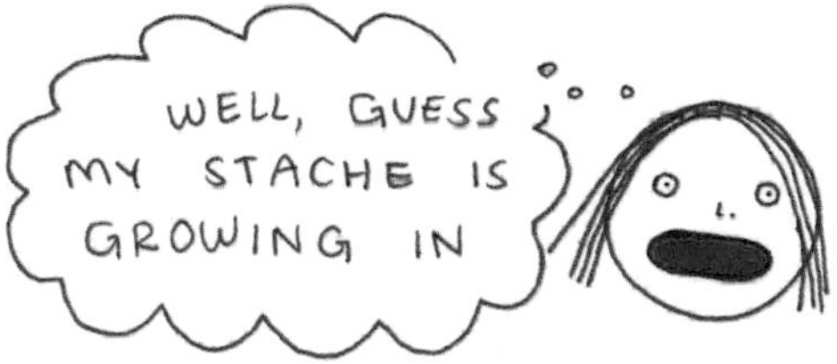
WELL, GUESS MY STACHE IS GROWING IN

I LOVE THIS BECAUSE THOUGH I CERTAINLY SUPPORT WHATEVER THE FUCK YOU DO / DO NOT DO WITH YOUR HAIR, I DID NOT - AT THIS MOMENT IN TIME - HAVE A MUSTACHE I WAS AWARE OF.

INTERNET OBSERVATION

TYPES OF PEOPLE YOU MAY MEET ON THE WEB

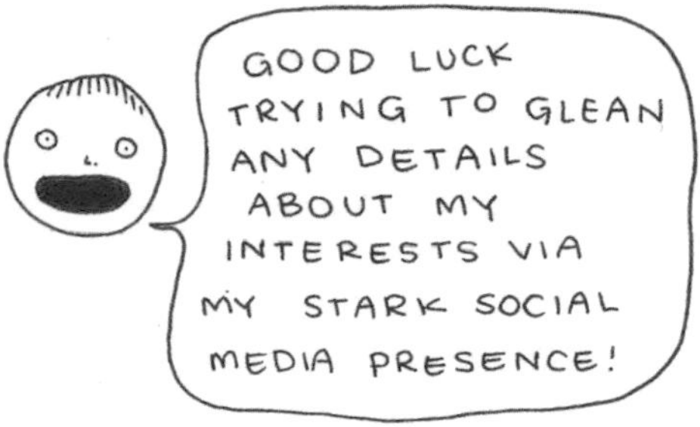
GOOD LUCK TRYING TO GLEAN ANY DETAILS ABOUT MY INTERESTS VIA MY STARK SOCIAL MEDIA PRESENCE!

GUY WHO ANTI-CURATES HIS FEED, MOSTLY HIS "ARTSY" PHOTOS OF TRASH, NEON, AND DOOR CORNERS

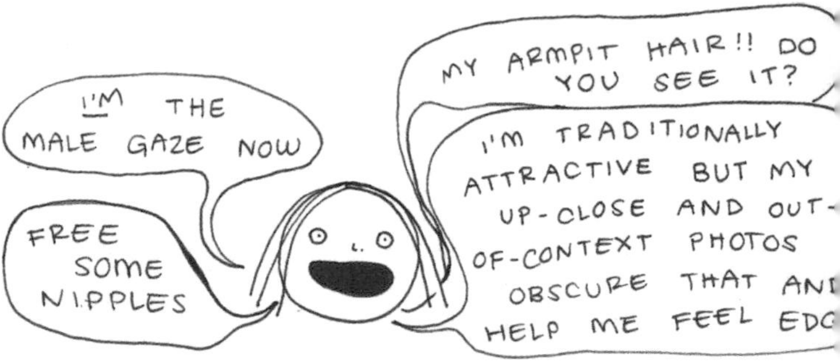
I'M THE MALE GAZE NOW
FREE SOME NIPPLES
MY ARMPIT HAIR!! DO YOU SEE IT?
I'M TRADITIONALLY ATTRACTIVE BUT MY UP-CLOSE AND OUT-OF-CONTEXT PHOTOS OBSCURE THAT AN
HELP ME FEEL ED

INSTAGRAM... ARTIST... WHO IS WHITE + THIN

HERE WE ARE AT A FJORD!

AND HERE IS THE SAME PHOTO ON MY ACCOUNT

COUPLE WHO ARE VERY
MUCH A COUPLE WHO CANNOT
STOP TRAVELING

WHO NEEDS THERAPY AND/OR GOOGLE WHEN I CAN ASK STRANGERS ONLINE TO WALK ME THROUGH MY MISINFORMED BELIEFS

THIS NIGHTMARE

REASONS YOU SHOULD DELETE SOCIAL MEDIA AS PROVIDED BY THE TECH MAN TURNED HUMAN TED TALK WHO CREATED THESE PROBLEMS IN THE FIRST PLACE!!

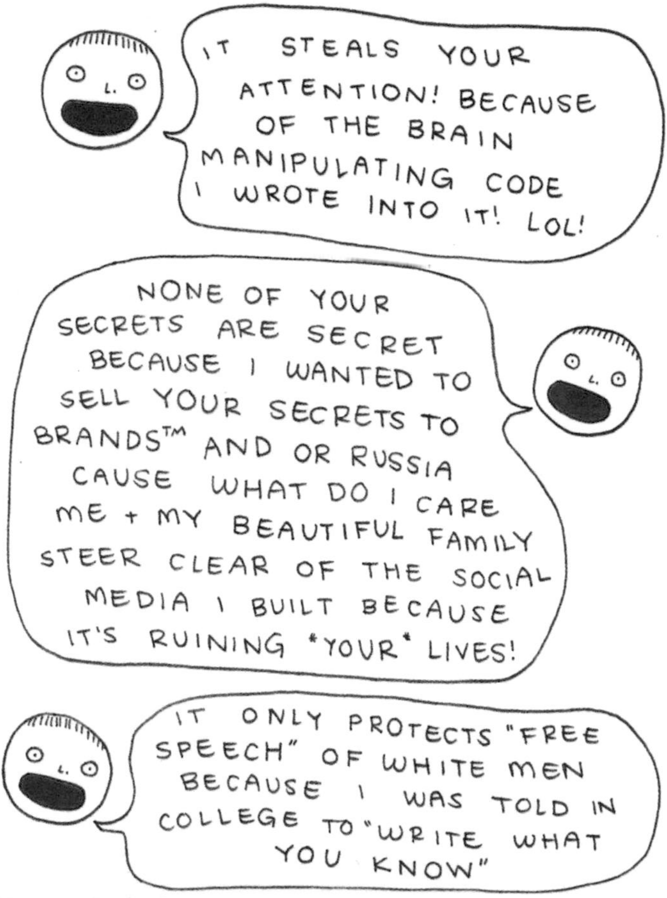

IT STEALS YOUR ATTENTION! BECAUSE OF THE BRAIN MANIPULATING CODE I WROTE INTO IT! LOL!
NONE OF YOUR SECRETS ARE SECRET BECAUSE I WANTED TO SELL YOUR SECRETS TO BRANDS™ AND OR RUSSIA CAUSE WHAT DO I CARE ME + MY BEAUTIFUL FAMILY STEER CLEAR OF THE SOCIAL MEDIA I BUILT BECAUSE IT'S RUINING *YOUR* LIVES!
IT ONLY PROTECTS "FREE SPEECH" OF WHITE MEN BECAUSE I WAS TOLD IN COLLEGE TO "WRITE WHAT YOU KNOW"

ACTIVITY SECTION

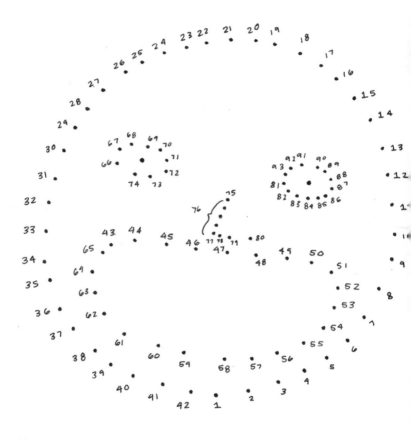

PAINT! BY! NUMBER!

COLOR KEY

1 = RED

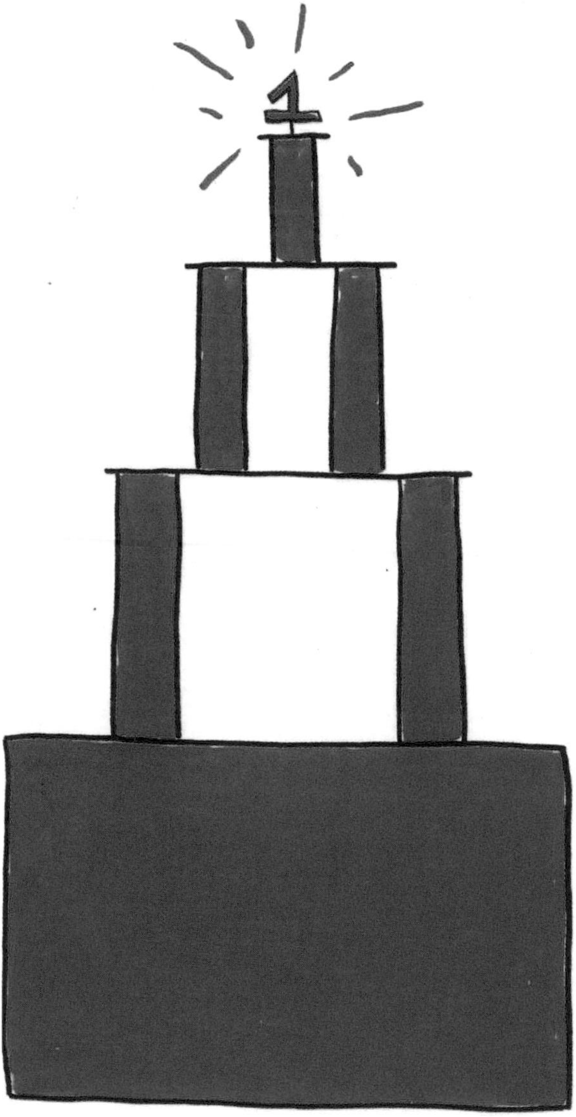
1

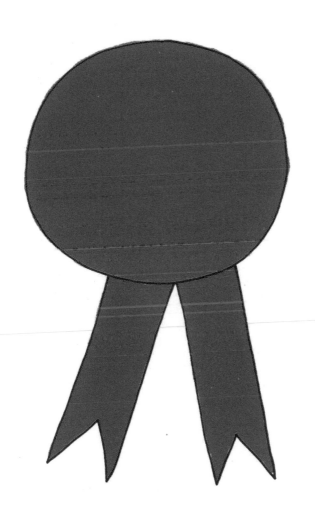

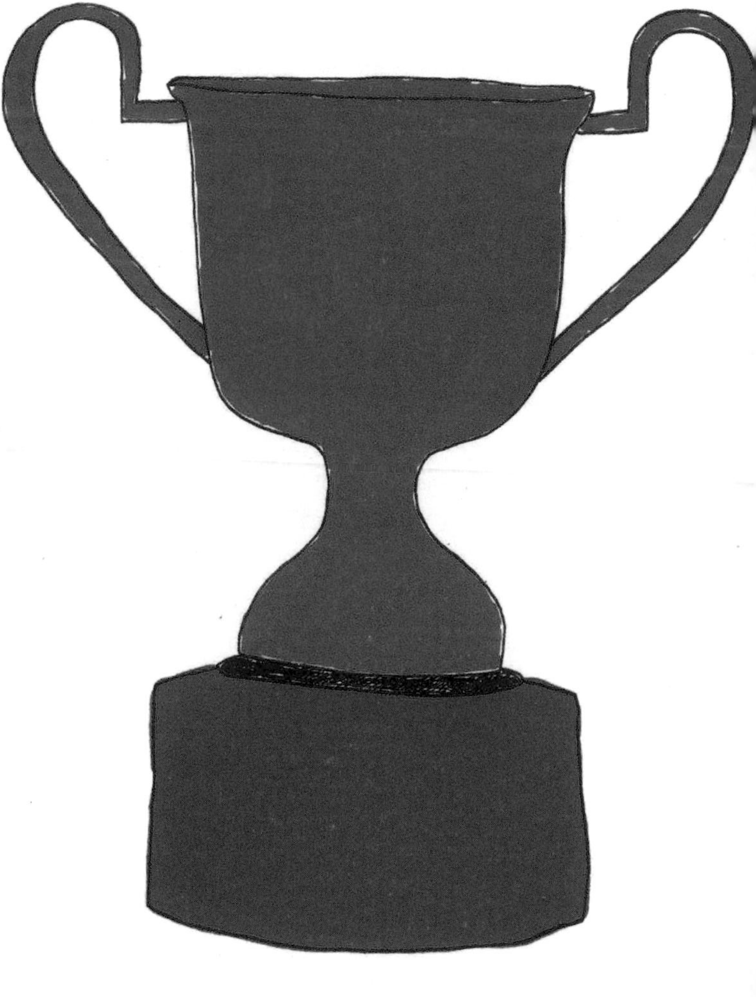

ACKNOWLEDGMENTS

How do you thank everyone who has made you what you are? You can't. So, here's an abridged version.

My family is an obvious start. They made me! Mom, Dad, Fleg, Emily, Deb, Shirl, and all the rest of you: you are the funniest, strangest, most loving, loudest people I have ever met. I wouldn't be who I am without each and every one of you, and I love you all so much.

To everyone at Penguin Random House, including Meg Leder and Patrick Nolan, THANK YOU. To my brilliant editor, Shannon Kelly—Shannon, you are so wise and wonderful, and working with you on this project still feels too good to be true.

Thank you to Sterling Lord Literistic, especially Mary Krienke. Mary, thank you for understanding not only the heart of this work, but also the peculiar nature of doing this work, and for being an amazing friend along the way.

This book and project would not be possible without the people whose thoughts indelibly shaped my own. To name a few whose words were essential to me on this journey: Rebecca Solnit, Mitski, Dr. Brittney Cooper, Rachel Cargle, Maggie Nelson, Angela Y. Davis, Rebecca Traister, N. K. Jemisin, Ursula K. Le Guin, and Ann Leckie.

Much of the thinking in this book started at Oberlin with Dr. Wendy Beth Hyman, under whose watchful and encouraging eye I learned about old men and their myths and the strange, gnarled relationship between words and things. Wendy, thank you for being such an incredible teacher, human, and friend. To all my teachers before college: thank you, especially Anna, Ben, Vanessa, Mrs. Tsap, Zach, and Julian. Thank you all for teaching me to write good, for being such brilliant thinkers in your own right, for the work that you do. You are teachers who change lives.

To the awards for good boys "community" online: there isn't enough space to explain. Know that I am deeply, deeply thankful.

To my beautiful, wonderful, weird friends: I love you. Thank you, and I'm sorry to those of you who had to endure years of me working through all this shit before I decided to funnel it into drawings. To those of you who saw this project when it was on a stack of 4x4 notecards that I kept in a hermetically sealed plastic bag: thank you for believing in this project when it was a half-formed mashed-potato mountain.

And to all the good boys I've loved—you didn't get me here, but I sure as hell wouldn't be here without you.